Hear what othe
Soozey Johnstone and *I am the Problem*

Soozey Johnstone has written one of the most intelligent, practical and deeply honest books that I have ever read. The complexity of being successful in a business of any size has been broken into overcoming 9 key obstacles. To do this will require inner contemplation, group engagement and some seriously honest conversations. The end result will be extraordinary. I can't recommend Soozey's book highly enough.

> **Andrew Griffiths, Australia's #1 best-selling small business author**

I'm loving the book! After having read it I now have it sitting within easy reach in the office and pick it up frequently. The insights it contains are easily accessible and always helpful. It is a great tool that helps me both in 'keeping it real' and in knowing that the daily challenges of management, which at times seem overwhelming, are not mine alone and that there is a way forward.

It directs me to self-reflection and pragmatic solutions to issues big and small. The processes for analyses are clear and immediately accessible as are the practical suggestions for good practice. In short it can be used for long term as well as day to day improvement.

> **John Molony, Executive Director, Deakin International**

Soozey has been my staff development guru for over 10 years and for very good reasons. I turn to her on my toughest assignments and she has never failed to deliver results. Soozey uses her energy, tailored approach and a deep understanding of human behaviour to awaken self awareness in those she works with. I am the Problem is an essential addition to your leadership 'toolkit'.

Darren Taylor, VP Internal Audit, Amcor Ltd

I am the Problem is an honest and pragmatic assessment of the human challenge with change — that we don't comfortably look to ourselves as the starting point. Every chapter in this book is a facet of the prism through which we must see ourselves in order to understand why we get what we get in life. With this perspective we can begin to change our self and the world around us. I am also the Solution…

Stuart McGregor, Partner, Hames McGregor + Partners

Soozey will tell you, "Its all about the people!" Having a clear mission, great strategy and attainable goals for your business amounts to nothing if your people are not engaged and willing to put their heart and soul into the business and own the outcome. Working in the technology space, we have many smart people, many of whom are introverted and quiet achievers. But often, we get in our own way of success. I have used Soozey in a number of my business ventures to break thru these barriers and to unleash the will to succeed! Read this book and give it to your staff …. it will be the best investment you ever make.

Trevor Townsend, Serial Entrepreneur

Soozey has a natural talent to quickly identify the issues and insights that are required to lead change in a positive manner. We have worked together to create a high performing team with its own 'ethos' and 'esprit de corps'. The experience gained from such an exercise enabled a new threshold to be reached for myself personally in the areas of Human Capital Management and strategic leadership.

I have subsequently used and built upon those very same principles in other organisations during my career.

Joe Locandro, Director Information Technology,
Cathay Pacific | Information Management | Executive Office

Soozey is one of those rare individuals who brings a positive perspective to everything she does. Impossible is not a word in her dictionary. She has an incredible ability to combine enthusiasm, drive and critical thinking to tackle even the most difficult business challenges.

She has mentored many executives and forced them to challenge the status quo in their careers. She supports people with a structured approach to achieving their goals and a tenacious attitude that holds them accountable for their commitments. Her perspectives are based on a wealth of real life experiences and an attitude that we should pursue our dreams and not settle for second best.

Soozey has helped me greatly in my career and she is one of the people that I trust most to provide me with honest advice and innovative ideas. She is a powerhouse of energy and positive thinking!

Mark Hamill, Group Manager,
Risk & Assurance at Fortescue Metals Group

Would you like to know what's holding your business back? Give a copy of this book to every member of your leadership team. On the inside cover, write the words 'Read this book and give me measurable feedback about how we can do better and I can lead better.' Then, start taking action on the responses that you get. It will be the best use of your time this year!

Claire Marriott, Managing Director, APAC Leaders

Soozey's methodology for business success has application for organisations of different sizes across different industries.

The small changes that every individual can make to improve communications, processes and break bad habits can have profound beneficial consequences and enable organisations to achieve their broader collective goals.

Soozey has developed simple but effective steps that every leader, or aspiring leader, can take to improve their own personal motivation and effectiveness — and that of the people around them.

The approach is not at all 'light and fluffy'. Breaking habits also means challenging individuals to make the tough decisions for both their personal benefit and that of their organisations.

Dan Feldman, Managing Partner, HR Legal

From the moment I first met Soozey I knew she was a special person. Soozey has a zest for life matched by a fierce determination to be successful at everything she takes on.

Her career has involved dealing with people from every walk of life, and a diversity of professions and industry. She has developed a deep understanding of people and personal motivations that is matched by very few.

Soozey has put these learnings into practice, getting the best out of people while guiding them through life and career.

It seemed natural for Soozey to extend her reach. Writing this book is her way of doing so.

**Glenn Fielding, Chief Executive Officer,
UXC Professional Solutions**

I found Soozey more or less by chance. Chatting to another young CEO on a domestic flight we found parallels in our companies — but there were distinct differences. His direction was clear, his team sounded cohesive and passionate: he had an unwavering trust [in] them. Most of all he was enthusiastic, focused and excited about the future and how Soozey was a major part of how he got there.

Engaging Soozey for me proved to be much more than just executive business coaching. This is managing people and personalities at a far deeper level to achieve goals that benefit everyone — not just the P&L. Understanding what makes your team tick is one part, discovering what makes you tick brings business and life beyond the office walls to a completely different level.

Simon Paull, CEO, Paull & Warner

I have watched Soozey Johnstone help transform successful business leaders into exceptional business leaders for over fifteen years. In *I am the Problem*, Soozey shares her expertise and insight into leadership and business success in the same way she helps business leaders daily — by being refreshingly honest, direct, humourous and always with integrity.

Soozey's insight into human behaviour is extraordinary. Now is your opportunity to spend time with Soozey with this great read. Get ready to learn and grow!

Jennifer Galvin-Rowley, Director, Galvin-Rowley Executive

Soozey' energetic, practical and determined approach is inspiring. She was able to create an environment in which I was able to challenge myself and to face my shortcomings in terms of leadership, communication and interactions with my teams. Soozey encouraged me to spend time reflecting rather than 'just doing' so that I became more effective in my life at professional, business and personal levels.

My first challenge was to reassess my attention and intentions — where should I focus my time and energy to achieve my 'Big Hairy Audacious Goal' (BHAG) for the company? This required me to really work hard on my time management and task prioritisation as well as my personal behaviours and communication style. Of course, this required me to challenge my existing mindset and to break through my comfort zones.

This personal work is critical to the success of effective change so I suppose I needed to change from the 'inside out'. I have a new way of approaching and living my life, and although it can be a daily challenge after two years I feel that I work smarter and live better.

Soozey encouraged me to examine my real purpose in life at a personal level so that I could clarify how I could best serve our customers and fulfil our mission and vision. This has been a life changing experience and I feel more confident and competent in my professional, business and personal lives thanks to Soozey Johnstone.

**Chris Mitchell, Chief Executive Officer,
Health Workforce Queensland**

As a small business owner and someone who has assisted many business people with their finances, I can highly recommend Soozey and her book *I am the Problem*.

So many management books talk the talk but never give you sensible, practical advice on how to walk it! Follow the tools here and see immediate improvement in your bottom line as it shows you how to actually get results … what a refreshing change.

Louise Lucas, CEO, Why Money Matters

Soozey is responsible for changing my life direction!

Soozey enabled me to better understand what I was really passionate about. I am loving my career assisting the poorest of the poor in fifteen nations by facilitating development projects, helping donors give wisely and seeing lives transformed! Soozey is a breath of fresh air in any business environment and her wisdom, insight and engaging style has guided me and many others to do what we love.

Richard Beaumont, CEO, Entrust Foundation

Any interaction with Soozey leaves you feeling energised and inspired with what is possible. She is the most natural marketer I have met and knows exactly how to get the most from a team.

She really gets business and couples this insight with a personal style that is engaging and empathetic to the person she is dealing with.

Tom Stianos, CEO, SMS Management & Technology

I'm a very visual person and not much of a reader, but I just couldn't stop reading, "I am the problem" by Soozey. Simple, practical but a powerful tool that enables one to step away from the daily management grind and self-reflect!

Indi Siriniwasa, Enterprise Sales Leader — Trend Micro, Australia & New Zealand

I just love this book. I have never read anything this carefully. I love the lengthy introduction: it reveals your authenticity. I have learned so much from you and about you and your approach. I'm reading it with the aim of being the person I need to be by the end of the book. I will be the change-maker in our business and shape the future with my team. I can see it now.

Julian Fraser, National Relationship Manager — Aviation QBE Australia

I AM THE PROBLEM

9 obstacles that suck away business success — and how every leader can overcome them

Soozey Johnstone
with Stephen Yolland

I am the Problem

Published in Australia by Method9: www.method9.com.au

PO Box, 290, Carlton South, 3053

ISBN: 978-0-9924585-0-8

Edited by Jo McKee
Design by Luke Harris, Working Type Studio: www.workingtype.com.au

For my father and mother.

And for my adored and ever-patient husband.

Contents

Thank You!

I have been planning this book for ten years — in my head.

In 2001 I was running a twelve-month program in
the Melbourne office of one of the big global consulting firms.

During that year, and specifically during those workshops and
coaching sessions, the book that you are now holding had its
genesis. So, the first person to thank is Darren Taylor, who was
a participant in that 2001 program, and continues to be such a
wonderful supporter.

Patiently, Darren has asked to read my manuscript every time that
we have caught up over the last ten years. Well, finally, here it is
Darren! Thanks for keeping me up to the mark!

I'd like to thank all my clients. Every single time I work with
someone, whether it's a strategy piece with an exec team or a one-
on-one coaching session, I'm learning. This is what I love so much
about my work — I'm engaged as the specialist, but equally I'm a
learner. Now I can share all my learnings in these pages. Oh, and
by the way, as you're reading the case studies you may recognise
your own story. A different industry and a different name … total
coincidence, of course!

The actual writing part has taken me almost three years. The most
important person on this journey over the past twelve months has

been my old friend Stephen Yolland — the whole world knows him as Yolly — who constantly inspires me to be courageous and write from my heart — to tell the truth without any fluff or 'consultant speak'. Yolly is a brilliant writer and editor. He is also a poet. He has an incredible, uncanny knack to turn pages of blurb into an engaging flow, seemingly effortlessly. But behind those twinkling eyes is such intense concentration: I have so enjoyed working on the book together.

Luke Harris continues to be one of the most patient people that I have had the pleasure of working with. And, I have certainly tested him over the last 18 months. I have lost count of the number of edits that we have made to the text and format but I know that it's close to 1,000. Luke has never shown any sign of angst and has been a serious contributor in getting *I am the Problem* out into the world.

And in recent months, the lady who has brought this ten-year journey to a conclusion is Jo McKee. Jo is a talented editor who lives in Queensland and spends most of her week sailing. There's something kind of warming and romantic about having my book edited in sunny Queensland. Thank you, Jo.

Thank you to Glenn Fielding, Donna Eiby, Susan Mackie and Alan Lachman for being courageous enough to lean into some curly conversations and provide me with the constructive feedback that would inevitably improve me, my communication, my self awareness and my confidence. As hard as they were, many of these curly conversations have been tipping points in my life.

After ten years of planning, three years of writing and 65,000 words, I started doubting myself and whether or not the book that you are now holding was any good. So, in that moment, I had a choice to make — put out an average book now or a great book later. And, the average-to-great gap required some reading and constructive feedback from Pat McIvor, Claire Marriott, Katherine Teh-White, Jen Galvin-Rowley, Louise Lucas, Lara Blamey, Lisa Montague, Stuart McGregor and my Dad, Peter. Between us, I think we've got to 'great'.

Throughout the writing journey I have participated in book-writing workshops with Robyn Henderson, Catherine Deveny and Andrew Griffiths whose generosity and support beyond our days together will be forever appreciated.

Thank you so much to Dr Carol Dweck, the author of *Mindset: The New Psychology of Success**. Carol is a world-renowned Stanford University psychologist who has been researching the topic of motivation for more than forty years. Carol, your research has changed the way that I think, communicate and coach. The best part is that your research has made me a better mum.

A BIG thank you to my brother Charles, Dad, my sister Heather and my mum, Joode. You have helped and supported me in so many ways.

To my beautiful Jim and my gorgeous girls, I just want you to know that you make every hour of every day exciting and fulfilling. You surround me with joy. I live with more enthusiasm, vulnerability and love because of you.

The Story Behind the Story

If you read this book — *really* read it — you will enjoy a happier, more productive and more successful life as you dramatically reduce the stress of owning or managing your organisation.

Then you can go home, hug your partner, kiss your kids, pat the dog and relax, content in the knowledge that you're doing your best.

That's what this book is about. Helping you to do your *best*.

I was born with a passion for business running through my veins.

Business — making things, creating things, building things — is part of the Johnstone DNA.

My grandfather, Charles, and my grandmother, Margaret, (who we grew to call Grandmeg), were entrepreneurs, buying Jellis Bakeries in Kew, Melbourne, and registering the business as a public company in 1937. They bought a further eleven bakeries throughout Victoria, and when Grandad died eight years later, Grandmeg carried the responsibility of leading the bakery, its eighty staff, and ensuring the customers were well served.

Dad tells the story as though it were yesterday: the pressure on him and his brother to miss school and help out with the bread run was combined with financial worries and uncertainty.

They made it through — Grandmeg was as tough as old boots. A woman who had very high expectations of both herself and others, I remember being a little terrified when she arrived at our place for Sunday lunches. She didn't talk much about the past but I have no doubt that those days were very difficult.

For me as a young child, hearing the family history, what struck me most forcefully was the massive sense of responsibility that Grandmeg, Dad and my Uncle John had for the families of the eighty people that they employed at the bakery. There was never any thought of doing anything else but working hard to ensure that the lives of those staff and their families would go on as normal.

Dad followed in his parents' entrepreneurial footsteps. At seventy-two, he's had twelve businesses over the years, mainly in the manufacturing sector. Most notably, Dad founded Wiretainers in 1970, making bread and wine crates. These days Wiretainers' expertise is in the design and construction of containers for the protection, separation and transportation of component parts used during the manufacturing process: stillages, trolleys, crates and cages, all made of steel, mesh or wire.

We didn't see much of Dad when we were growing up. He'd be off to work before we woke up and often home after we were asleep. I remember hearing Dad's car pulling up in the driveway and wondering whether tonight he might be a little happier.

Now I understand that the pressure of business — the hours, the money, the staff, the customers, the travel, the suppliers, the paperwork — all of it combined to wear Dad down a little more each day.

The times I loved the most were our annual trips to Lakes Entrance where we would be cooped up on a houseboat for a whole week. I noticed a lightness to Dad's demeanour. There was nothing better than watching the sun rise in the middle of winter over the crisp cold waters of Lakes Entrance. Just me and my dad, a few fishing rods, the sounds of the wind in the dry grasses, water lapping up against the side of the boat and the line being pulled by an unsuspecting fish. Nothing better.

Back then we never discussed it though. Why those times were better, and sometimes, wonderful.

In later years I gained a better understanding of the pressures Dad endured as I was growing up. My drive to help business owners and managers to create a culture that will ensure sustainability, flexibility, great profits and a lot of family fun along the way is born, in part, of the recognition that those early years with Dad could have been gentler, happier and probably more productive. I don't waste time with regrets and I have enormous respect for what Dad has built. I'm just thankful my life experience has been helpful to many others during my career. I know Dad isn't alone in the pressure he faced and in the way those pressures affected his ability to relax. So many people I know who run enterprises seem to spend at least some of their time downright grumpy.

Dad still works full time. Mind you, he doesn't have to. My brother and sister work in the business and growth over the past ten years has been healthy. I know, however, that Dad enjoys the sense of pride of being part of something successful that's driven by the family. He can get very emotional when he talks about it.

I've written this book for two main reasons: to combat the 'downside' to running an organisation and help people feel less grumpy while dealing with the pressures every business faces, and assist people to maximise their sense of pride in achievement. I love to see people learn how to make organisational goals easier and less stressful.

While tapping away at the keys I have mainly been thinking about the departments or businesses that I love working with the most. They typically have 30-80 staff, and a committed, hardworking and frustrated leadership team. They're at the stage where the team leader (or if they're a medium sized company, the CEO) is on the verge of a breakdown, executive relationships are fractious, valuable members of staff are choosing to leave the business they once loved and revenues have stagnated. These are the businesses that eat up my methodology, and push through the hard stuff to change the status quo.

That said, the methodology outlined in this book can be applied to organisations of all shapes and sizes. As you will read in the case studies, the majority of businesses or teams that I have worked with have at least 50 staff, although using the same methodology in businesses as small as 15 people has been extraordinary. I guess it's because when you make a change or two to a small business, the impact is very immediately obvious. Using the methodology in very large businesses works brilliantly as well, but experience shows us we need to have the ear of a sympathetic very senior executive who really 'gets' what we are trying to achieve and why, so we can leverage his or her authority when dealing with middle-rank managers who may be suspicious or threatened by outside consultants wanting to uncover both positive and negative things about the corporate DNA.

Using the proven techniques in this book you'll make it easier to overcome blockages in your own behaviour or management style

4

— blockages of which you may not even be aware. You'll unleash a culture of productivity and success throughout your organisation.

I must admit my personal 'sweet spot' is those second and third generation family businesses that aspire to continue into the third and fourth generations, providing an ongoing vehicle for both family security and prosperity for the country.

If you're a family member with those intentions, let me know! Share what resonates with you in these pages, what you implement, what you learn and what changes you see as a result. You may even find your story turning up in book two.

But every business matters. Some of Method9's best work has been done in massive corporations.

Whatever type of organisation you're involved with, you'll find my emphasis is on how we co-operate. This book will teach you how to ask yourself the questions that will ultimately improve your leadership style and mitigate the risk of you being the problem!

Please read this book with an open mind. The contents are the result of twenty years of chipping away at the coalface, keeping my eyes and ears open.

This is refined knowledge, rooted in the real world, tested and reliable. Use it.

With love,
Soozey Johnstone | Melbourne, January 2014

How To Get The Most Out of
I Am The Problem

I have always been an avid reader of business and professional development books.

In fact, I have often been teased by those closest to me over the years for never taking time out to read a trashy novel or magazine, and always having my nose buried in the latest self-improvement top seller.

The simple fact is, I have always found the theories of business and professional development really engaging. I read my first Dale Carnegie book when I was fifteen and quickly went on to read Napoleon Hill, Brian Tracy, Bob Proctor, Edward de Bono, Michael Gerber, and the list goes on and on!

I'm constantly amazed and humbled that I can pick up decades of a person's knowledge, wisdom and experience for under thirty dollars and — if I concentrate — I can learn what they've learned. And how to translate that learning into positive action.

Because the biggest challenge with any book is that it actually changes nothing, unless the reader chooses to change something.

The reader. You.

Words without action are meaningless and I will be the first to admit that I have read plenty of books with the intention of taking action — instead of the conviction that I must take action this day and the results were entirely predictable.

Nothing happened.

Maybe I wasn't ready for change. Maybe I was busy accumulating knowledge. Maybe the timing wasn't quite right. Maybe I was scared, or lazy.

Whatever the reason, I have thought long and hard about how we can avoid you falling into the same trap. To help you take that crucial step beyond simply reading what's in these pages and to get you to actually *act* upon them.

So, in writing this book it's my aim that you take away one good outcome from every chapter and I've structured the book in such a way that you will achieve this as an absolute minimum.

Each of the nine obstacles starts with 'The bird's-eye view of the chasm' — the chasm that exists between management and the workers, or between one manager and another, or between the Board and the executive team — and gives you an easy-to-follow solution to some of the potential cracks, gaps or even chasms you may well be experiencing in your organisation.

Each obstacle discusses how those chasms arise, and finishes with the 'Chasm closers' — these are immediate actions that you can take to reduce the likelihood of a chasm.

As you read, choose one 'Chasm closer' — the one action that you think is going to make the biggest difference to you and your organisation.

When you've chosen an action, discuss it with your leadership team and see if they agree with you that it's a priority. Start by implementing concrete action before moving onto the next section. Don't try and make too many changes at once.

And above all, get started. Begin. Now. It doesn't need to be a major action. A little win, a starting point, a decision to change the status quo and cut through the noise is what matters. And when you've bedded that 'Chasm closer' down, try another.

Always remember: done is better than perfect.

An asterix indicates notes or references throughout this book that are listed at the end, as an aide to further reading and research, as well as an acknowledgement of the people I have quoted. You will also notice many acronyms. If they become a little overwhelming, I have included a glossary on page 305.

I'm a big believer that books come to us for a reason. Certain books jump out at us on the book shelf or are given to us at the right time.

This is one of those books. It's now time to take action. If you're still in the bookstore tossing up whether to buy this book, then buy it. If you're about to start reading, then decide to translate the wisdom you find here into action.

It's a sad fact that many people — perhaps most people — will read this book and do nothing. But some people will read it and go on to transform their lives and organisations for the better. For these people, the phrase 'OK, good, so what now?' is second nature.

Never forget: 'What now?' Because 'What now?' is always your choice.

Obstacle 1: Self Awareness

A bird's-eye view of the chasm

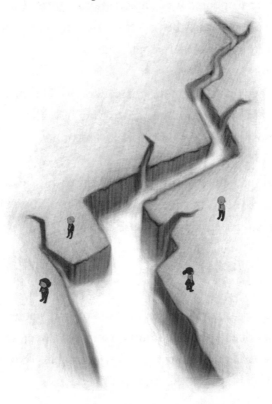

The hardest fact of all is that your success is ultimately limited by your biggest weakness, and your biggest weakness is usually the one that no one dares to tell you about.

But true leadership is about being aware. You're more effective when you're able to observe and control your responses.

Often, *how* you do something is more important than what you do. As the old cliché goes, actions speak louder than words!

The saddest (and most common) piece of management speak: what we have here is a failure to communicate.

Have you ever wondered why organisations continue to employ people who are obviously behind the pace, not contributing, or actively 'white anting' other people's efforts?

I have a theory that the majority of leaders would rather let performance and revenues slow down than have the hard conversations with their fellow leaders and staff.

In my experience the majority of problems in any organisation, when you pick them apart, are simply communication problems. Yet we let them fester. Why? Because often these conversations mean we have to tell someone how they are perceived by others. And that can be very uncomfortable. For you. For them.

We often see organisations where the majority of people are giving lip service to honest communications between them, but smiling sweetly at behaviour that is unacceptable. They're ignoring behaviour that is against the values of the business.

On one side of the chasm we can have a leader with their entrenched behavioural habits, such as poor listening, fluffy communication, too direct, too soft etc., and on the other side are the people who play the subordinate role and suck it up rather than rock the boat.

It takes incredible courage to give your boss or your peer some unrequested feedback.

And it takes real maturity for a leader to ask others for feedback on how they're perceived, and more importantly to implement that feedback, or to get some help.

Because of the chasm that exists between what we say and what we *really* think, people rarely, if ever, give each other feedback that will assist in improving their relationships, their work and their lives.

It's just plain awkward. It's easier to leave things left unsaid than to courageously and vulnerably state your view and assist a colleague with some constructive feedback. And, of course, the ultimate leader, the executive team member or the CEO, gets little or no constructive feedback at all. Sometimes even when they ask for it!

On one side of the chasm you have the employees who are so frustrated by a manager's lack of clarity, the slapdash impulsive decisions and the constant changes that don't seem to derive from any calm strategy. And on the other side is a manager who wants what's best for the business and the staff, who works long and hard every day, whose driving motivation is to get results, and who can't understand why everyone doesn't see the world the way that they do.

We have all seen this chasm. Chances are, if you picked up a book entitled *I am the Problem* you have a feeling that some cracks with chasm potential may be emerging.

Of all the chasms, this is the hardest to look at with unblinking determination. Why? Because when your direct reports feed back

13

to you, it's rare that they will tell you the whole story for all the obvious reasons — their future, their relationship with you and the impact that the feedback may have on the business. There's a little voice inside their head that justifies maintaining the status quo rather than telling the whole truth.

This can be the most important chasm to close because responsibility for every chasms begins at the top.

As you read on, keep this thought front and centre. Great leaders in any field demonstrate introspection, self-awareness, and deliberate encouragement of, and listening to, feedback.

The feedback chasm

Close your eyes for a moment and think back to the best boss that you ever had. What did you like most about them? Was it their ability to achieve extraordinary results? Their persistence? Their focus? Their ability to prioritise? If you could boil it down to just one word, what would it be?

Now think about your worst boss? Why was he or she so bad? What was it about their style that bothered you? Why?

It's easy to spot great leaders. They're the ones who are spoken of with enthusiasm, who the masses swarm to when the teams get together. They're the people who have something to say that others want to hear. They're often quoted and they have an incredible capacity to get things done, to deliver results, and to make a measurable difference.

It's just as easy to notice the worst bosses. From a first meeting with them they're complaining about anyone but themselves. Bizarrely, these people can often appear extremely upbeat and positive and yet they have an uncanny knack of slipping out the door when the finger-pointing begins. They are often too busy criticising others to do a good job themselves. One of my friends calls them 'smiling assassins'. I think we all know managers like this.

Which category do you fit into for your staff? Are you up there with the best or down there with the worst? Are you somewhere in-between? Do you know?

Earlier this year I was invited to assist with a merger. I started by interviewing the leadership team to understand the challenges in merging these two successful businesses. Every member of the leadership team spoke poorly of their current CEO. They had some positive things to say and yet it was his limiting behaviours that seemed to be holding the business back.

I asked whether anyone had bothered to provide the CEO with feedback. The responses were revealing, and predictable.

'Well sort of. I have told him that people are dissatisfied.'

'Yes, I have mentioned that he needs to refocus priorities and take more time with each of us.'

'No, I'm too old to be looking for another job. Who'd hire me?'

'Yes, I told him that things needed to change but I don't think that he was interested in hearing me.'

'Why would I bother? He's not going to change.'

With each piece of the feedback puzzle I found some common themes. Most members of the team weren't game to provide constructive feedback to their manager because of concerns that their relationship may be damaged. Secondly, the feedback that *was* given lacked clarity, examples, support and measurement.

Don't think that this was a first-time experience for me either. Almost every time I'm engaged by a CEO, direct reports take the opportunity to tell me (an external consultant) about how the CEO could do their job better.

Time and time again, I see the communication chasm widening as we speak. Especially when I ask the question 'What are the top three areas in which your CEO could improve performance to expedite the success of your strategy?'

Well, I suppose I am leading the witness, to be fair. But in my experience every direct report can answer this question. But do you think that they would ever bother to give their boss the feedback? Eighty per cent of the time, the answer is 'No!' But why? That's easy. Fear of threatening the boss, damaging the relationship, causing disharmony within the business, losing their job, missing a promotion. The list goes on.

And yet, choosing *not* to provide the feedback is inhibiting the success of the business and driving a bigger crack in the chasm between the CEO and everyone else.

The lonely CEO

On a recent four-hour flight, I happened to be sitting next to an exhausted man who turned out to be the CEO of a public company.

He opened up for three hours and spoke about his major challenges which all, essentially, came down to this: it's lonely being the CEO.

You do your best to involve others in major decisions and yet ultimately, it's up to you. The Board are great at a strategic level but they're not involved enough in day-to-day stuff. He went on: direct reports have a job to do and are responsible for their own departments. They don't involve themselves in the decisions that matter in other silos. Ultimately, it's the lonely role of CEO that carries the biggest responsibility. He's in the helicopter on his own; who can he ask for advice?

If you're relating to this, what are you going to do about it?

What would you like to do differently? To help you along the way, here are some recent answers to 'What are the top three areas in which your CEO could improve performance to expedite the success of your strategy?' These have been collected from a bunch of organisations that I have worked with.

- Clarify what we're doing.
- Stop talking and start listening. No, start *hearing* (because he pretends to listen).
- Stick at one thing. Stop moving our targets.
- Take time to understand me and my priorities.
- Get to know the staff better.
- Smile occasionally — look as though you're enjoying yourself.

- Learn to trust the leadership team.
- Be here more.
- Involve us in decision-making on expenditure.
- Let others solve the problems. Stop micromanaging.
- Manage your time better.
- Get some anger management training.
- Ask for involvement from the leadership team before making changes.
- Let me use you as a sounding board — don't always try and solve the problems for me.
- Be a role model for the leadership team by working more sensible hours.
- Share a bit about yourself personally. Who *are* you?
- Take the time to say hello.
- Be present when we're talking. Take the time. Look at me.
- Have some fun occasionally. Come along to drinks on Friday night.
- Take other people's ideas seriously. Provide feedback.
- Understand the difference between being consultative and getting things done.
- If you think something's a waste of time, still show interest.
- Tell us what we need to change to work more effectively with you.
- Trust me.
- Explain the thinking behind the decisions.
- Involve us more in decision-making.
- Stick at the plan that we have agreed.
- Don't tell, SELL.
- Consult the leadership team before giving directions to staff.
- Be aware of the way you behave under pressure and the effect that it has on the business.

- Tell us why we're here. What's expected and how we measure success.
- Be clear.
- Follow through.
- Let us learn from our mistakes. Give us the chance to fail occasionally.
- Let others have a voice.
- We need a clear vision.
- Stop acting on the advice of external consultants. We (the leadership team) have the answers.
- Stop playing favourites.
- Improve clarity in communication.

And the list goes on, endlessly. Note how many of these relate to communication.

The other side of the chasm — why attitude, skills and experience are not enough

Every comment on the list above has come from people within organisations we have worked with: the majority of whom enjoy their work, their colleagues, their environment and yet they are still suffering on the other side of the chasm.

And tragically, the majority of people would rather leave the organisation than address any of these challenges with their manager.

Here's the thing.

You have worked so hard to get to where you are. You've spent time at university, time working your way up the corporate ladder, time taking extra skills-development training, time learning from your consultants, lawyers, accountants, time learning about the business and the industry that you're in. And, yet what if there was just one crucial limiting behaviour inhibiting your success?

What if *all* of the effort that you have put into your career and your life up until this point isn't enough to get your business more profitable, to get your staff happier and more engaged, to increase your revenues? What if this is it? The brick wall?

Yet, what if the potential answer to your current challenges (and the reason that you bought this book in the first place) lay in the answer to a few simple questions? Would you be interested?

You would? Great!

Then the starting point is to get some feedback on yourself as a leader: your strengths, your limitations, and your critical areas for development.

In my experience, the most efficient way to do this is through using a 360° feedback tool*. The best tools that I have found are those that provide a number of answers (as drop down box options) to each question rather than giving the employee or colleague an open opportunity to comment.

The 360° process will assist you in prioritising the critical areas that are going to have the biggest impact on your success.

When choosing a 360° feedback tool, find a tool that's behavioural-based rather than competency-based. Why? Because ultimately it doesn't matter how high your competency level is, if it's your *behaviour* that is blocking your success.

When choosing people to rate you for your 360° review, use a combination of peers, subordinates, clients and key stakeholders — at least five of each. The more raters you have, the more valid and robust your feedback will be. Choose raters who you know will be constructive but honest. You're after courageous, useful answers.

Ensure that your 360° feedback report is reviewed with someone who has a deep understanding of the tool and has the expertise to align your learning outcomes and actions to the strategic objectives of the business and measure your success.

What's really interesting to me is that it's often what we consider our greatest strengths that ultimately become our biggest limitations — if we let it happen. Here is an example:

CASE STUDY

Simon is the CEO of a manufacturing business. He's a people person in every sense of the word. He focuses on ensuring that everyone is happy, engaged in what they're doing and that they enjoy coming to work every day. Everyone loves Simon. In fact, if you were to meet many of his staff for the first time, it wouldn't be unusual if the first thing you hear about is how much they admire their CEO as a person.

When meeting Simon for the first time, we quickly got to the challenges in the business. He was losing sleep over business growth. The business had stagnated and revenues had slumped consistently over the previous two years. It turned out that in putting people first, Simon had created some significant challenges in the business such as people working part time, working from home, on different salary package arrangements, some were paid for study, others weren't, etc.

From the outside in, it seemed that all of Simon's business decisions were made as a reaction to what the staff wanted.

When I lifted the rock and interviewed people across the business in depth I found a huge chasm between the CEO and many of the staff. Although they *liked* him, it appeared to many staff that Simon had his favourites and that some of those so-called 'favourites' treated other staff poorly and took advantage of the CEO's generosity.

A them-and-us culture had grown up between corporate services and service delivery, there was a lack of formal measurement and a lot of mediocre performance.

In a business of eighty staff, this problem should be easy to fix simply by coaching the CEO to put the business first. In putting the business first and making every decision in line with business growth, Simon would be making the best decisions for the staff.

Simon's first major task was to bring the leadership team together and let them know about his desire to be a better leader and his request for feedback.

The result of his 360° degree feedback was no surprise to me.

John Wiley & Sons (the Everything DiSC® 363® for Leaders* surveyors) encouraged Simon to consider the following statements.

The three critical areas in which Simon had to focus were:

1. **Communicating with clarity.**

    a. You may find that it's sometimes difficult for others to understand you.

    b. You may struggle to put your thoughts together before communicating.

    c. Because you like thorough information, you may spend more time than necessary explaining things to others.

    d. You may not always remember to clearly state the topic before you explain your points.

2. **Stretching the boundaries.**

    a. You may be reluctant to give up the current way of doing things if people seem to like it.

    b. You may fear that people won't like you if you push them beyond their comfort zones.

   c. You may see little need to stretch the boundaries as long as conventional methods are getting the results you need.

   d. While you may appreciate innovative and creative thinking, you may feel that you just don't have time to explore new territory.

3. Communicating about problems.

   a. Because you don't want to ruffle anyone's feathers, you sometimes let inefficiencies slide.

   b. Because you dislike conflict, you may gloss over problems rather than address them directly.

   c. Because you don't want to hurt people's feelings, you sometimes hesitate to speak up when there is a problem.

Once he had his feedback, Simon and I clearly determined performance measures for each of these critical areas in line with his three year business strategy. From there Simon started working on his thinking, behaviours, daily planning, communication, processes and best use of energy each day.

Within twelve months, the business had increased revenues by twenty per cent despite the fact that we had to reorganise teams, re-structure some of the service lines and even replace some of the leadership team.

What's the value of a 360° degree feedback survey to Simon? About $2.7 million!

If you are going to spend serious dollars on professional development, then I would like to challenge you with the thought that often the best place to start would be to increase the self-awareness of every member of the leadership team *and* — AND! — transparently SHARE with each other, courageously, those critical areas that each member of the team needs to work on to increase the success of their division or department in line with overall strategy. Don't let the 360° feedback turn to mouldy dust on the shelf. Throw a dinner party, open a decent bottle of red, and read each others' evaluations.

See, I'm a believer in keeping things simple. The fish rots from the head. And when it rots, it stinks up the whole place.

Don't bother investing millions in the professional development of your staff and ignore the absolute requirement for the management team to function expertly and efficiently.

To improve the functioning of your organisation, *start* with you and your leadership team. Head to head and toe to toe, agree to act on the three critical personal behavioural areas that are going to give the organisation every chance of success. Commit to sharing the results, and thus increasing your self awareness and the awareness of your colleagues so each of you are taking action each day in those areas that require attention.

I am well aware that there is a school of thought that suggests that we shouldn't concentrate on our limitations. Instead, we should work to our strengths and continue to build on them. There is an element of truth in this but you need to first understand whether your limiting behaviours are also limiting the business's success, and which of your positive behaviours make the most difference.

25

Feedback from and within your leadership team will help you and them to focus on good behaviours and reduce bad ones. As a result, and increasingly, your day-to-day activities will more closely align to successfully executing your strategic plan.

Don't go it alone. If every member of the leadership team gains further insight through 360° feedback and shares their TOP 3 development areas, and the actions that they're going to take, you can all courageously and vulnerably support each other on the path to achieving greater success for yourselves and your business.

Sharing the TOP 3 development areas

Jennifer was the head of sales for a global IT infrastructure firm. She was brilliant in sales. The CEO had headhunted her from a competing firm and her nickname was Missy Million because she rarely brought in a deal under one million dollars. I received a phone call from the CEO one day that went something like this:

'Soozey, we have an issue with turnover in the sales team. Ever since Jennifer started working here, she's been leaving behind her a wake of crying account managers and resignations from administration staff. Hell, even some of the blokes are unsettled. Now, I like Jennifer. She's like me. She gets things done and she's bloody great at what she does. So, I need to work out a way of keeping her here with no more tears and no more resignations. Also, I need the admin team to get out of the bathroom and back to their desks!'

Jennifer had been on many professional development sales courses but she had never participated in 360° feedback. The results spoke for themselves.

Jennifer's greatest learning was that she didn't always need to have all the answers. In fact, her role as a leader was to create the space for others to have a voice. Yes, to her clients, Jennifer was the 'problem solver'. In the office Jennifer was the 'people leader'. Behaviourally, these roles are very different.

Initially somewhat confronted, it took her a couple of weeks to realise that the feedback was one of the greatest gifts that she had been given in her career.

I will never forget the moment when Jennifer looked at the differences in the feedback from her clients and the feedback from her subordinates and said 'I just have to think from the moment that I wake up every day, that if I respond to my staff the way I currently respond to my clients, I'm going to love my job much more.'

Within that moment, Jennifer's self awareness increased exponentially. Sure, she still loses the plot occasionally when under extreme pressure (apparently especially in the tender writing process) but it's much rarer these days and everyone around her is much happier and more productive.

Sink thinking and swim thinking

OK, you've got your 360° feedback. How can you successfully use the information within it to your advantage?

Ponder this for a moment. It is your thinking that creates your environment, your reality, your world. YOU are the sum of your thinking and all of the decisions that have led you to this stage in your life.

You have a choice how you think — positively or negatively — in any given situation. I call these two thinking choices 'Sink or Swim Thinking'.

Do you control your thinking? Do you influence your decisions? Have you made a conscious plan getting to this point or did it just happen?

Thinking *does* just 'happen'. We make 50,000 decisions every day and the majority of these decisions are unconscious or automatic. Most of these decisions fall into a daily pattern: for example, we always get out of bed on the same side, eat a certain cereal for breakfast, drive the car to work on the same route and have lunch at the same time every day. (It's actually a psychological state called 'Repetition Compulsion', but that's another story.)

Sometimes something out of the ordinary jolts us out of our routine such as road works holding up the traffic so we have to take a different route, or maybe a song on the radio triggers a happy memory and gets us grooving and singing on our way to work.

This change in our routine, however minor, affects our thinking, our outlook, our energy levels, our attitudes, our behaviours, and the way we choose to manage our time through the rest of the day.

You arrive at the office and a colleague, who hasn't even had a conversation with you yet, says 'Hey, you are particularly perky this morning.'

These 'out of the ordinary jolts' don't come along all that often when we are comfortably stuck in our routine, but they come along more regularly when we have a clear goal that we want to achieve, with a written plan to support it. Because our every action is conscious and has a purpose, we become more alert and aware of the opportunities and ideas around us that can help us to our goal.

If you become more 'conscious' over a long period of time you will find you form new thinking habits, giving you greater control of yourself, ultimately resulting in you controlling your thinking rather than your thinking controlling you. For example, take the case of an enthusiastic entrepreneur who is always buzzing around, always eagle-eyed, looking for new business activities or investment opportunities. It's what turns him on. Needless to say, as he is constantly looking for them, because he expects to find them, he finds them. That's how it works. We are what we think about.

Over the years, I have found that a significant percentage of clients have self-limiting beliefs about their ability to succeed. In fact, just about everyone has them in one manner or another. It will be well worth your while giving some thought to your self-limiting beliefs and why they exist. Then, restate each belief with a solution-seeking question. For example:

Sink Thinking: 'I've never been involved in a merger before. This is way outside of my comfort zone. I am going to mess this up.'

Swim Thinking: 'I've never been involved in a merger before. How could I increase my knowledge? Who could I speak with who has succeeded with a merger and could mentor or support me through the next two months?'

Use this 'Sink or Swim' process to challenge your self-limiting thinking at an activity level. For example, consider the following scenario:

Goal   To increase revenues by twenty-five per cent this financial year.

Activity   To achieve all the success measures for the merger.

Situation   Two members of the leadership team have resigned due to the impending merger. You arrive at the office and another member of staff shares their concerns about communications regarding the merger.

Sink Thinking: 'I'm not in charge of internal communications, don't know where to start, so I can't solve this problem. So I am probably not going to achieve the targets that I have agreed with the Board.'

Swim Thinking: 'I'm not in charge of internal communications so I'd better find out who is and get to know them fast. I reckon we can improve the clarity in communication and optimism throughout the business if we're intentional about it.'

So, out of the 50,000 thoughts that we think every day, how many are good for our motivation levels and how many are bad? The trick to improving our motivation levels is to ask ourselves the questions that will give us *positive* answers.

You perform better when you're happy. Simple as that. And as your happiness is determined by your thinking, your thinking is a critical determinant of your success — so think about it!

> *People who cultivate a positive mind-set perform better in the face of challenge. I call this the 'happiness advantage' — every business outcome shows improvement when the brain is positive. I've observed this effect in my role as a researcher and lecturer in 48 countries on the connection between employee happiness and success. And I'm not alone: in a meta-analysis of 225 academic studies, researchers Sonja Lyubomirsky, Laura King, and Ed Diener found strong evidence of directional causality between life satisfaction and successful business outcomes.*
> —**Shawn Achor, *The Happiness Advantage: The Seven Principles that Fuel Success and Performance at Work****

Success? It's all in the mind!

> *Your life is an expression of your mind.*
> —**Lawrence Olivier**

The daily news is full of the stories of leadership failures. But conversely, the way in which we measure and recognise success in leadership appears steeped in mystery.

When I started as an executive coach fifteen years ago, my focus was primarily on the personality, values and beliefs that ultimately drive leadership behaviour. These days scientists and researchers are able to watch the brain at work using FMRI machines (functional magnetic resonance imaging). Combining research using this advanced technology with more traditional studies is fundamentally changing the way in which we view leadership, management and business. And what have we discovered?

- Some styles of feedback (positive or negative) may not actually improve performance because they do not 'light up' the pleasure centres of the brain.
- Many people are not particularly motivated by their next salary increase.
- The majority of people are motivated by engaging work in which they have the opportunity to learn, grow and connect.
- Celebrating, recognising and rewarding many small wins is more successful than focusing on the big wins.
- Many leaders do not *really* believe in personal change.

I mentioned earlier Dr Carol Dweck's book, *Mindset: The New Psychology of Success**. A world-renowned Stanford University psychologist, Carol has spent more than forty years researching the topic of motivation and says that our achievement is determined by whether we approach our goals with a 'fixed' or 'growth' mindset. Dr Dweck's research divides the world into 'learners' and 'non-learners'.

The fixed mindset sees talent as a non-developing trait: it is what it is. It doesn't grow or adapt according to circumstances. The fixed mindset is self-handicapping and does not offer a recipe to recover from failures. The growth mindset sees talent as essentially learnable.

The growth mindset cares more about learning than getting a particular result or achieving the goal. It capitalises on mistakes and confronts deficiencies. With a growth mindset, nothing restrains future potential.

Or to put it as our mothers might have taught us, 'Try, try and try again' — using what we have learnt to increase the likelihood of success, of course.

The mindset of leaders can permeate values, relationships and activity throughout their organisation. So the question becomes: do you know whether or not you are fostering a culture of learning — of the growth mindset — within your business?

According to the work of Peter Heslin, Associate Professor of Management at the University of New South Wales, fixed mindset managers do not welcome feedback, are not good mentors, do not recognise and reward others' success and are not open to employee growth or change.

If that sounds like you, don't despair or fire yourself. The great news is that mindsets can be changed. It's a choice.

A growth mindset, led from the top down, will have a significant impact on your culture and your revenues. How? By adhering to some simple rules outlined by Dr Dweck:

- Presenting skills as learnable
- Conveying that the organisation values learning and perseverance, not just ready-made genius or talent

- Giving feedback in a way that promotes learning and future success
- Presenting managers as resources for learning

Without a belief in human development, many corporate training programs become an exercise of limited value. With a belief in development, such programs give meaning to the term 'human resources' and become a means of tapping enormous potential.

How to Grow Your Mindset

(with thanks to Dr Carol Dweck, from
Mindset: The New Psychology of Success*):

- Are you in a fixed-mindset or growth-mindset workplace? Do you feel people are just judging you or are they helping you develop? Maybe you could try making it a more growth-mindset place, starting with yourself? Are there ways you could be less defensive about your mistakes? Could you profit more from the feedback you get? Are there ways you can create more learning experiences for yourself?
- How do you act toward others in your workplace? Are you a fixed-mindset boss, focused more on your power than on your employees' well-being? Do you ever reaffirm your status by demeaning others? Do you ever try to hold back high performing employees because they threaten you?
- Consider ways to help your employees develop on the job: Apprenticeships? Workshops? Coaching sessions? Think about how you can start seeing and treating your employees as your collaborators, as a team. Make a list of strategies and try them out. Do this even if you already think of yourself

as a growth-mindset boss. Well-placed support and growth-promoting feedback never hurt.

- If you run a company, look at it from a mindset perspective. Think seriously about how to root out elitism and create a culture of self-examination, open communication and teamwork. Read Lou Gerstner's excellent book *Who Says Elephants Can't Dance?** to see how it's done.

- Is your workplace set up to promote groupthink? If so, your whole decision-making process is in trouble. Create ways to foster alternative views and constructive criticism. Assign people to play the devil's advocate, taking opposing viewpoints so you can see the holes in your position. Get people to wage debates that argue different sides of the issue. Have an anonymous suggestion box that employees must contribute to as part of the decision-making process. Remember, people can be independent thinkers and team players at the same time. Help them fill *both* roles.

Old habits die hard

Habits are comfortable, and they are automatic. And annoyingly, that goes for both good *and* bad habits.

Habits start in the mind, and turn into behaviours. 'It's raining; I won't go to the gym today' is a thinking habit that turns into a habit of not going to the gym in the winter. Three months pass.

How do you go about replacing the old, comfortable, nurturing reflexes with something challenging, new — uncomfortable! — conscious and ultimately more rewarding habits?

To change your habits, first recognise that they exist, and secondly turn the unconscious and automatic into conscious and thoughtful. Think about John, for example:

CASE STUDY

John is a forty-year-old entrepreneur who describes himself as being inspired by the new, easily bored with the status quo, and a motivator. I am working with him right now.

He has acquired three businesses in the last five years and appears to be highly successful: great staff, long term clients and contracts, excellent revenues and an awesome culture across all of his businesses.

Even though things look rosy on the outside, John has a major challenge that he is grappling with on the inside. He has 'lost his mojo'. John still jumps out of bed each day, has an hour at the gym and is in at the office by 8:30 am but from the moment that he arrives, he finds it painstakingly difficult to motivate himself. He thinks he can't fix it. It's become his new norm. His very lack of mojo has become expected, comfortable and habitual.

Earlier today, John read his business goals to me over the phone, as though he was reading the back page of a newspaper he wasn't very interested in. *Nothing* that he was working towards was lighting him up. All of his goals were predominantly finance, administration, and process driven.

The crux of the problem? He was lacking a big, personally meaningful goal and concentrating (at an activity level) on the things that didn't suit his passions or his behavioural style. His business had grown to a point where his role as CEO had become a firefighting, reactive 'job' and he couldn't see a way out.

So, what does John need to do to break out of his new status quo? Start by determining the things that he enjoys the most and then work out how to get more of those things into his day. Another acquisition is not on the cards right now although there are many elements of the acquisition process that John really enjoys such as the research and negotiation that could be incorporated into his day, aligning to a 3-5 year plan and a longer term personally meaningful goal. John's biggest challenge in making this happen is to trust his direct reports in taking on more responsibility of the day-to-day running of the business.

This is a challenge for many entrepreneurs, by the way. The opportunities that really light up their world are the big deals, the next acquisition, potential partnerships and alliances. It's so important to mix it up and always have a few serious goals on the horizon.

Our thinking habits — our default settings — have a tremendous effect on our productivity, our performance, our motivation, our happiness, our income, our relationships, our lives. If we let them!

Do you feel it's time to start changing some of your thinking habits? Or your behavioural habits? Or your communications habits?

I will be the first to tell you that it isn't easy. The amount we spend as a society on dieting and gyms, while we become steadily fatter and less fit is testament to how difficult people find it to change their lives.

The really interesting thing is that as your habits change, so too does your brain. In effect, you can re-wire yourself. So, if you are like John and don't quite understand why you're not responding to your environment the way you'd like to, explore your habits — the ones in your head, and the ones in your life.

Here are some good tips:

1. Increase your self-awareness. At the same time every morning, think about the habit that you are working on and write it down. Reinforce your desired modification by asking yourself a positive question about it. 'How will I benefit if I think/do this?' Choose to try and keep your new habit front of mind throughout the day. (See 'Memory triggers' below.)
2. In the evening, spend a few minutes to reflect on your day. What worked well and what could be improved in modifying your habit? Do this every day for thirty days and thirty nights and watch the dramatic difference.
3. The moment that you have any negative thinking, block it out by re-stating the negative as a positive question. Not 'Damn, I didn't get a chance to talk to Bill today and now he's in the air. That's the project derailed for another week.' Rather, 'What else can I do besides talk to Bill to keep the project moving?' Repeat this re-stating process as often as it takes until you have a positive alternative.
4. Be open with other members of your leadership team about the habits that you are working on, and how dealing with

them will align to the continued success of the business. Ask them for feedback on behavioural strengths and areas for improvement.

5. Use memory triggers as reminders. For example, use stickers that are particular for the behaviour or habit that you are working on. Put the stickers in obvious places such as the fridge door, front door, steering wheel, inside your wallet, on your diary, in your handbag, on your desktop, etc. Every time you notice a sticker it will jolt the memory of your new habit or behaviour. Even the most successful people continue to do this!

I have found that the best way to change a habit or form a new habit is to use all of these five tips *in unison for 30 days without a break.*

This is all about being vulnerable. It's about considering how you feel, what you think, how you respond. These are not activities that are consciously part of our business day, but nevertheless our thinking determines our responses and our ultimate success.

Does this all sound like too much effort? Well, what if these simple tasks could increase your profitability by two per cent and your revenues by twenty-three per cent in the next twelve months? Worth trying? This is the result one CEO I worked with saw.

I am not naïve or mindlessly enthusiastic. I do understand that this is the most challenging part of this book. But if you truly seek success then tapping into those 50,000 daily thoughts and taking note of the way you think is unavoidable because if many of those thoughts are negative, they will be affecting your self-esteem, your outlook, your productivity, your communication, and ultimately your revenues and profitability. Equally, positive change — change towards what you *really* want in your life — begins with positive thinking.

I have read a couple of wonderful books this year that will help you better understand how habits work: *The Power of Habit: Why we do what we do and how to change* by Charles Duhigg*, and *Making Habits, Breaking Habits: How to Make Changes that Stick* by Jeremy Dean*. And remember:

> *All our life, so far as it has definite form, is but a mass of habits.*
> **—William James, 1892**

The benefits of journaling

In case you haven't guessed, I have a particular interest in the latest brain science research. The reticular activating system (RAS) sends a strong message to your cerebral cortex **when you write things down.** Using pen and paper. There are many reasons for this.

There is a thoughtfulness that comes with handwriting that doesn't come as easily when using a keyboard. You connect spatially to your pen and paper and move through a process which involves more conscious thought than using a keyboard. You can't write at the same speed as you type, so you go more slowly, which equates to more thoughtfully. In short, the connection between the task and brain is stronger.

Getting you away from your desk, away from the office environment, away from distractions to writing, reinforces this thoughtfulness. It's about reflection, planning, innovation and possibilities. To help you to think differently, it's important to create the environment to assist you in doing just that. I could go on, but I know that if I had to hand-write this book and post it to you, it would be a different book! Maybe, just maybe, it might be a better book.

Recent research explains the benefits and the impact that journaling — writing down your reflections on the day — has on your mindset.

Journaling allows us to pause and consider consciously the positives and negatives in our day. It affords us the opportunity to reframe our day in our minds to our benefit. And it's one of the simplest ways to cultivate a positive mindset so we can perform better in the face of challenges.

Journaling is a great way to train your brain to achieve the 'happiness advantage'. To find out more about this research, buy yourself a copy of *The Happiness Advantage* by Shawn Achor.

Chasm closers

Grab a big sheet of paper. Just start writing:

What would you choose to do differently if you were more present, more conscious and if your daily actions were consistently aligned to strategy?

What are the TOP 3 areas in which you could change your thinking and behavioural habits to improve performance and expedite the success of your strategy?

What strategies can you put in place immediately to keep you focused on those TOP 3 areas every day?

Let your mind wander. If you consciously manage the way in which you choose to respond to your environment, what will change? Write it down.

What would happen if you became conscious enough, in the moment, to respond out of a choice in line with your strategy, instead of responding habitually?

What change would have the single biggest impact on your personal and professional success? How would this impact the business? Can you put a measure on it?

How can you learn and grow those skills which will make you more effective as a leader?

What is one professional challenge that you're currently facing? How could you approach your challenge with more of a growth mindset?

> *Leadership is scarce because few people are willing to go through the discomfort required to lead. This scarcity makes leadership valuable. It's uncomfortable to stand up in front of strangers. It's uncomfortable to propose an idea that might fail. It's uncomfortable to challenge the status quo. It's uncomfortable to resist the urge to settle. When you identify the discomfort, you've found the place where a leader is needed. If you're not uncomfortable in your work as a leader, it's almost certain you're not reaching your potential as a leader.*
> **—Seth Godin, *Tribes: We Need You to Lead Us***

Obstacle 2: Strategy

A bird's eye view of the chasm

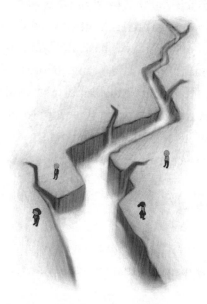

How often is the 'S' word used in business?

Strategy.

We hear it constantly. It comes up in endless meetings, memos and corridor conversations. More time is spent musing on 'strategy' than almost any other element of business planning.

We all use the 'S' word as if it was well-understood or easy, but how many of us actually succeed in delivering meaningful, successful strategic change for our organisations, consistently and easily?

Time after time, strategies are only partly successful; they become side-tracked, they wither and die.

Why? What's the gap between what we're *doing* and what we're supposed to be achieving?

Well, I am here to tell you that most of what we hear in our organisations, what we say to each other, what consultants sell us, what we *believe* about strategy is basically bunkum. Because after half a lifetime consulting to a vast range of organisations I have determined that there's one really important word when it comes to strategy. And instead of placing this word front and centre in our deliberations, it's something we often forget to consider, or we merely pay lip-service to.

The word is *Clarity*.

'Whoa!' I hear you say. You've invested your hard earned money in my book, and my insight is that you need *clarity*?

Yes. Because twenty-five years of front line experience in a vast number of organisations convinces me that clarity is the one thing most corporate strategies lack. And without clarity — not just for us, but for those who we manage — the most insightful and well-planned strategy is inevitably doomed to fail, sooner or later.

Let's have a look at the clarity chasm.

On one side is the dynamic, focused leadership team who are enthused about the strategy and their individual responsibilities in achieving it. On the other side sit all of the workers — the implementers. Often, very few people on both sides of the chasm know that a chasm even exists. Everyone *appears* to be very busy getting stuff done.

Whenever I mention clarity, leadership teams are always vehement that they *are* clear about what they're doing, where they're heading and how success is measured.

But if I walk fifteen paces from the Boardroom in which we are having the conversation and ask a staff member in an open plan workstation about how their role and activities *align* to the strategy, they usually can't give me a clear and immediate answer. Or, even any answer at all.

Honestly, I see it time after time. Big organisations, small ones, public, private, community, government — doesn't matter. Strategic clarity usually ends at the Boardroom door.

Clarity? We talk the talk. We don't even know how to begin to walk the walk.

Yes, the staff often understand their job description based on preconceptions from their previous job roles, their interview process, how they feel they are going to be measured, and so on. But they might not understand — at all — how their performance translates directly into the strategy that the executive team members have carefully hammered out.

(By the way, back in the Boardroom, now that the external consultant has popped out for a moment, a heated discussion has ensued about whether they *are* clear about strategy at all. Half the team has lapsed into silence, and the other half are wrestling with each others' opinions. But that's another story, for another book. Let's assume, for today, that we *have* a strategy.)

One of my clients is a successful, highly-respected but rather old-fashioned law firm. Believe it or not, they still employ a tea lady. (Actually, he's a tea man!)

Now imagine if he delivered cold tea to the Boardroom for a crucial client meeting, served in chipped cups, and without a welcoming smile or polite word to those he is serving. A tea man? Most people would consider his role to be least important in the implementation of that firm's growth strategy. But believe me, in that moment, he is *central* to the customer's experience — crucial to the revenue growth of the firm. He's part of the pitch. So he needs to see his role as more than just a guy who makes tea. If he does his job well, he plays a key role as a custodian of the firm's customer-centric culture.

To do this, he needs clarity on his role, and why it is so vital. Does he even know who the client is? If the visitors were, say, the owners of a local football side, would he know to murmur congratulations on their win at the weekend? I am sure you take my point.

The client would suddenly feel special. 'Even the tea man knows who I am, and cares about what I care about.' These are the 1% moments. These are the few words or supportive actions that transform our workplaces, and, in turn, ensure that strategy actually 'happens'.

So why is clarity between leadership teams and those they lead so hard to achieve, and so difficult to spread throughout an organisation?

The relationship between organisational strategy and any individual's daily actions may be clear in their role description and KPIs, but how close is it to the corporate strategy — especially if it's just changed, or developed — if we were to actually measure their work activities on an hourly basis?

The sad answer is, often, not very close at all.

On one side of the chasm is a well documented, clear and measurable strategy approved by an executive team and the Board. Each person involved is glad to see the thing ready to go because the effort in getting to this point was arduous and time-consuming.

There have been some healthy debates and a few back-and-forth discussions between the CEO (the middle man), a risk-adverse Board populated over-heavily by lawyers and accountants, and the entrepreneurial executive team.

Highly-reputed external consultants were involved in aspects of the strategy development and perhaps auditors cast their critical eyes over the financials.

OK, maybe some debate still continues, but we *have* a strategy. Time will tell if it's the right one, but you know what? 'Done is better than perfect', and procrastination is the enemy of business success. (Of any success, actually.)

So here we go, all guns blazing … implement the strategy! Right?

But wait a moment. On the *other* side of the chasm sits the staff.

The staff who are going to actually *execute* the strategy and bring the business closer to its vision day by day.

Their sense of pride and happiness at work revolves around feeling part of something bigger than themselves.

Their understanding of the impact of their work on the business is crucial to sustainability and ongoing success.

They might be the 'tea man' at any given moment. So — seriously. Ask yourself this one crucial, life-defining question. Right now.

How clear are your employees — day by day, and every day — about what they're supposed to be working towards? *Really?* I mean each and every employee, in their personal job role. Of the difference that they *personally* can make?

Because the answer to *this* question determines the *size* of your strategy chasm.

And the size of your strategy chasm determines your success or failure. Simple as that.

But hang on, before we try and fix that, because I haven't finished taking pot shots at 'strategy' as a concept. Clarity is just one problem. There are others.

Strategy? What strategy?

Plans are useless, but planning is everything.
—**Dwight D. Eisenhower**

Something that has always baffled me is the very idea of *strategy*.

I remember in my early days in the corporate sector when executive teams would go away for a few days to work on strategy.

It sounded so incredibly official and challenging.

One year, an announcement went out to all staff and we were given the opportunity to write to the executive team (this was before the days of email; yes, I am *that* old) and share our ideas in preparation for their annual strategy session.

Being an enthusiastic twenty-something with big ideas, I spent a full Saturday writing about the opportunities that I could see in the market and how we could potentially achieve even greater success.

I still remember how excited I was writing my strategy letter which finished with the observation and comment, 'As a new member to the business, I'd be really keen to better understand what we're working towards.'

Ah, the naïve hopefulness of youth.

Needless to say I never received a response from any member of the executive team and, just as predictably, I never bothered to follow up or spend any more time providing feedback. Although it was delayed a while, my inevitable departure from that organisation began that very day and, when I did leave, with me went all my skills, enthusiasm and knowledge.

See, I didn't realise it at the time, but that experience was a tipping point in my working life. I share it with almost every new client I work with.

'How many young Soozeys are sitting in your office, struggling to be heard, right now?' I ask.

Why was it so significant for me? Because up until that point, I innocently assumed that the responsibility of strategy development sat with the decision makers at the top of the business. So, their very obvious lack of interest shocked me.

But being something of a go-getter, I refused to let the lack of interest dampen my personal enthusiasm. Because no one ever told me that junior staff didn't do such things, I wrote my own strategy.

Having always been a goal-setter, I used a very simple process to devise a plan for my division that, unbeknown to me, would see me promoted to GM status within two years.

Having a plan — and sharing the plan as the business grew — was incredibly engaging. To me it made the long days feel short and the hard work fun. I knew that I was onto something.

But in quiet moments, I got to wondering why *everyone* didn't work this way. It seemed so ... obvious.

So the next step was to get everybody in my team together and share ideas about the future.

You know what? Some people within the group had wonderful ideas.

In fact, the most innovative ideas would often come from the most interesting places — often the administration team, actually. Or they would come from new people, who weren't 'hidebound' by the knowledge that 'We've never done that before.'

The admin team? Sure. Pointy-headed questions such as 'How could we go about measuring the cost per potential customer to sale versus the cost of new business within an existing account?' went on to become essential measures of our success over time.

The business grew to $11 million over two years and then the cracks started to emerge. Cracks such as recruiting under pressure and making rushed decisions that detrimentally impacted revenues.

Again, we took stock, got together as a team and took the 'strategy' concept further: drilling down to the questions 'Why are we here? What do we want to achieve? What's in it for me?' Knowing full well that we all needed to become more effective and efficient, we entertained the idea of a profit share for everyone.

The profit share idea was a revelation, and a revolution.

It came from a member of the team who said they'd like a pay increase for the extra hours they were putting in.

After discussing the idea with the whole team, we agreed on revenue targets, profit targets and putting aside a percentage of profit for team profit-share.

The percentage of this profit-share given to any one individual was based on performance, and the performance criteria were determined by each individual in the team.

For example, for the receptionist, performance measures included timeframes and delivery of certain tasks, specific measurable feedback from colleagues, and resulted in a fifty per cent reduction in the number of calls that went to voicemail by creating a back-up system with another team member.

For each team member, we had a one-page measurable agreement which was clearly aligned to our monthly, quarterly and annual business performance measurements, and to our financial performance.

The following quarter, we exceeded our targets — you knew that was coming, right? — and decided to take the whole concept one step further by asking the question 'What are you spending your monthly profit-share on?'

This was the most exciting part. Now, even though I'm sharing a memory from 1998, I remember many of the individual goals that we shared.

There was a trip to New Zealand, tiling the laundry, visiting Paris, a new dishwasher, landscaping the back yard, exploring Indonesia, and the most amazing one (from the girl who 'wasn't a morning person' and didn't know that she could improve her moods) was a $500 pair of Bally shoes!

You should have seen the spring in her step each day as she saw those shoes becoming a reality!

As a team leader, I no longer asked how the numbers were going. Work became so much more interesting when I asked 'How's Paris going? Are you getting closer today?'

Additionally, there were metaphors sitting on desks, photos on screensavers and dialogue that was personally focused.

When we hit $18 million in Year 3, I really knew that we were onto something.

More importantly, we all loved coming to work.

I remember one of my best friends saying to me over dinner 'Soozey, I'd give anything to talk about my work the way that you do about yours. How did you find something that you enjoy so much?'

I was stumped. I couldn't answer that question then, but I can now.

It wasn't really *work*. It had become a communal effort towards a shared vision, a goal that was personally meaningful and lots of fun. In fact, it was so rewarding that I still look back on those years as some of the best in my life.

Hard work, great fun, personally meaningful work, awesome people, transparency with the numbers, giving back and an opportunity to learn and grow. What else *is* there? Really, what else?

So: what do all these happy memories have to do with the 'S' word, again? Well, we were forced to make our own strategy because our leaders failed to communicate theirs, and we made it anything but 'foggy and fluffy'. We rooted it in what was meaningful to each individual, day by day, and the part they were playing in achieving the overall target. It was hugely successful.

Imagine if this success had been created by our leaders, and replicated throughout the organisation?

So this is essentially what I'm saying! Twenty years later I can see clearly what made those days so engaging and energising.

Strategic alignment + personal meaning = successful strategy implementation.

Those years were the impetus for me establishing Method9 in 2001 and now I am privileged to share what I've learnt with businesses and organisations, from start-ups to global corporations, across a variety of industries.

Organisational success can be as simple as taking the fog out of strategy and aligning individual goals to organisational intent — and I do mean every hour of every day.

Interestingly, if you asked twenty-five year old Soozey about what strategy is and what it means to business success, she would have said that it's a very large document that's carried around in a big three-ring binder, it's owned by the leadership team and it contains a map of the future.

So what would I say if you asked me now?

The talking stuff

Strategy is *not* a three-ring binder sitting on a senior manager's shelf.

It is actually an on-going *dialogue* between management and every individual member of staff.

It requires constant tending, it is part of the fabric of daily communication that helps every individual to determine the best use of their time in any given moment, in line with the over-arching business vision.

Strategy helps us to communicate, delegate, prioritise, challenge and debate.

It gives all of us a voice — if we want to have one.

The stuff that gets affected

Good strategy — strategy that is clearly defined, and understood at all levels of the business — helps us to recruit well.

It helps us innovate.

It makes our decision-making easier, and reinforces the importance of flexibility in our problem solving.

It helps us achieve change, with less stress and more chance of the right outcome.

It helps us work smarter: it guides us to establish meaningful day-to-day benchmarks that we can review to see how we're tracking, and it directs our activities for tomorrow.

Critically, it helps us head off mistakes before they occur and sometimes it prevents disasters.

It's everyone's stuff

Strategic understanding needs to be in and part of every one of us. That way, it enables us to make a difference, to have a say, to feel valued as we contribute to something far greater than ourselves. The value of this cannot be over-estimated, and I will talk about it often in this book.

It helps us to understand each other, to motivate each other, to care and contribute to the success of our team, our division and the impact that our business has on the world.

And it creates the 'stickiness' that helps us to *keep working* and make the world a better place.

Good, clear strategy is the *only* way to grow a business consistently.

Mahatma Gandhi sums up my concept of strategy in one of my favourite quotations:

The ocean is composed of drops of water, each drop is an entity and yet it is part of the whole, the 'one and the many'.

The BHAG

When talking strategy with clients, I like to challenge them with the idea of the Big Hairy Audacious Goal, otherwise known as the BHAG (pronounced BEE-HAG), to which the strategy aligns.

The BHAG was originally proposed by Jim Collins and Jerry Porras in their book *Built to Last: Successful Habits of Visionary Companies*[*] and it should be the basis for all smaller strategies, tactics, projects and goals that any organisation may have.

The idea behind the BHAG is that it is a single 10-30 year goal; it is challenging, meaningful, audacious, clear, measurable. It is communicated and owned by the whole organisation.

By making the timescale a minimum of ten years, the organisation is instantly focused on two key facts: (1) this is not about 'playing around the edges' and (2) it will, in all probability, outlive the current participants.

We are planting oak trees here. We may never see them grow to fruition. BHAGs can be shorter — sometimes conditions dictate that they be so — but then we should perhaps call them something else, or think hard about whether they really *are* our BHAG.

Having a BHAG — even considering what one might be — encourages compelling and visionary strategic objectives. Collins and Porras describe the BHAG as an 'envisioned future'.

A true BHAG is clear and compelling, serves as unifying focal point of effort, and acts as a clear catalyst for team spirit. It has a clear finish line, so the organisation can know when it has achieved the goal; people like to shoot for finish lines.
 —**Collins and Porras**

Making a BHAG 'happen'

So if you're going to have a strategy, start by determining your ten-year BHAG and work back from there. Below are some questions to assist you with the process.

And yes, these questions are challenging. They're meant to be. (Just have a go!) (Oh and by the way: BHAGS are as good for one-person businesses as they are for massive multi-nationals.)

1.   Spend thirty minutes writing the answer to 'Where are we heading over the next ten years and what's the vehicle for getting us there?'

Then:

2.   Describe the next five years for your organisation — come up with a smaller BHAG (a SHAG, perhaps, if that doesn't make you blush) — that aligns to your ten-year BHAG, and then break it down into a year-by-year plan. Bullet points are fine. Be as specific as possible. Share a story. Describe everything from staff to offices to you and your role, clients, processes, financials, challenges, achievements, feelings — just write. Don't think too much, just write!

3. What are the responsibilities of each member of the leadership team in ensuring that the vision is delivered? Please write these down, including your measures for success. (Either individual measurements — Key Performance Indicators — or how the organisation will look when 'success' is achieved. Or both.)

4. How does your answer to Q3 *currently* impact on Q2 and how would you like that to change — if at all?

5. How will each of your leadership roles evolve over the next five years, in line with Q2?

6. How will you hold each other accountable? How will you get out of day-to-day operations to give this some time and reflection? What has to change?

7. What leadership challenges are each of you responsible for that are going to take the business to new heights?

8. What changes, small or large, can you make *immediately* to expedite the business's success?

9. Who is ultimately responsible for the following?
    -   Getting the strategy and structure in place that creates consistent growth in line with vision and purpose?
    -   Creating a culture of responsibility?
    -   Providing advocacy for the plans?

10. What reasons can you identify already for why the BHAG is doomed to fail? Could they stem from, for example, personnel, resources, or an external pressure?

Once you have answered these questions, ask other members of your leadership team to do the same.

Then, spend at least a day offsite sharing your results and seeing where the disagreements lie. Decide on a timescale for agreeing upon a specific, measurable plan that reflects the goals.

It might be a good idea — no, strike that — it is *always* an excellent idea to have this session chaired independently to ensure that no one individual (or idea) dominates discussion, and that all the key points are analysed, thoroughly discussed, and captured.

Now it's time to get each of your business unit managers to go through the same process with each of their teams, using your BHAG as a starting point.

The benefits of going through this exercise are amazing. In fact during a recent review session with a new client, we asked them what the benefits had been in working with me and my team. He smiled and said 'You had me at the questions. Answering the questions as an executive team has transformed the way we think.'

Here's another recent email on the BHAG topic.

> *What's exciting about our BHAG is that our language within the Partnership meetings has started to change. I now understand how incredibly important language is. Now that we are talking about our revenue targets as a measurable plan, we can really see the reality of being on track to our ten-year target.*

In this customer's case, the BHAG was broken down and measured through quarterly financial targets. But the measure isn't always financial. It could be about market positioning or market share. It could be changes to your manufacturing process.

It could be product development. It could be anything which gives you a competitive advantage, or it could be a strategy to 'float' the business or buy your biggest competitor.

With this customer, here are the immediate actions that were taken after the first BHAG planning meeting:

1. More detailed and forensic accounting to provide a clear understanding of where they are at, plus the implementation of new financial models.
2. Each partner was tasked to present their plan at the next partner meeting.
3. Accounting was tasked to build a resourcing budget into cash flow modelling.
4. A decision was taken to employ a sales manager to put performance alignment processes and communications in place so that staff clearly understand that reaching 70% of a target is not OK.
5. The sales team was boosted by 25% by the end of June.
6. A determination was made to reduce cost-driven decisions and use a business case process for budget approval.
7. They decided to hire a marketing specialist full time.

Any one of these actions could have made a substantial improvement to the organisation's bottom line. From a full-hearted and courageous BHAG meeting, they implemented all of them.

Don't be afraid to uncover your BHAG. A really exciting BHAG is transformative, so it should be the start of any strategic review, even if you think you know what your BHAG is already.

During a presentation at the Skoll World Forum, Roger Martin, the author of *Playing to Win: How Strategy Really Works** and Dean of the Rotman School of Management at the University of Toronto in Canada, made an incredibly important point. He said:

> *Every model is wrong and every strategy is wrong. Strategy in a way helps you learn what is 'righter'. People think you can prove a strategy in advance. You can't.*

In other words, strategy is always our 'best guess', and it is never set in stone. The world changes — sometimes very quickly — and the implementation of our strategy must be flexible enough to work around those changes.

Strategies are, by their nature, moving feasts.

For that reason, your people must understand strategies fully and bend their activities to what meets the needs of the BHAG, not just respond to the day-to-day pressures around them.

When I have asked individuals to track their activity over thirty days and then align that activity both to their personal KPIs *and* the strategic plan, the response is always cringe-factoringly shocking.

I think that this happens for one or more of the following reasons:

1. Advancement (or simple job retention) is based on attending to KPIs, but these are often historic (not responsive to the rapid organisational or market pressures that people face) or they are poorly drafted to begin with. An employee who is focused on their KPIs to the detriment of achieving the

BHAG is badly advised, badly led, and probably going to be a victim of the fallout when the organisation reviews its overall performance.

2. Instead of a one-page strategy that everyone in the business understands, the 'strategy doc' is fifty pages long and collecting dust on some manager's shelf. The staff don't know it, don't understand it, and do not chart their course according to it.

3. The leaders don't translate the vision in a way that's meaningful for those who report directly to them and *their* direct reports suffer as this omission is passed down the line.

4. Performance measures are not clear enough at a team level and may not be aligned to the BHAG at all.

5. Communication and measurement don't happen on a regular basis: the most senior leaders go away each year to discuss strategy but they don't have the ability (or make the time) to build strategy performance measures into the fabric of daily business communication.

6. With the best of intentions, the original strategy gets overshadowed by a new business opportunity that may not necessarily be conducive to the BHAG, but which may provide useful revenue or exposure.

7. Last, but by *no* means least, employees and middle management see the senior management saying one thing and doing another. This instills mistrust, apathy, and an inability to align.

This gap between the desires of management, their inability to lead and the behavioural responses of subordinates is responsible for more business failure — and more sideways or backwards moves in people's careers — than any other factor.

Regardless of why it exists, the strategy chasm can be significant.

Closing the chasm starts with the ability to create a powerful, meaningful shared vision and then bring it to reality through people and ideas, throughout every aspect of your business.

It requires, as I like to express it, a leadership team with a cool head — to do the real intellectual grunt work to define what the BHAG is, and also a warm heart — a leadership team that actually believes that empowered, independent-minded, self-responsible employees who are aligned to the vision is the only way to achieve it.

Leadership: a vehicle for great visions

Great leaders inspire people because they understand the needs and motivations of others and can effectively communicate their vision. Indeed, great leaders are the *vehicle* for great visions and, thus, create the environment and conditions for true motivation to flourish. So here are some thoughts on leadership.

Leadership is more about who you are than what you do.

Leadership is complex, but it can be learned.

Leadership always requires courage, clarity, imagination and passion. Self-interest should be the smallest part of a manager's desire to lead. Sadly, it is often the largest part, and some organisations mistakenly encourage this view of the world.

Leaders need to be resolute, able to persevere through hardship and setbacks. They must be bold and daring if they are to aspire to personal and organisational excellence.

Leaders are results-focused and are recognisable by their achievements.

Leaders understand that success is rarely created alone.

Leaders are powerful and persuasive negotiators, internally and externally.

Leaders attract and retain talented employees and colleagues and turn talent into achievement through their shared vision. Their teams always feel that they are part of something significant, something that makes a difference both to the real world and to them as individuals.

Leadership requires total personal responsibility. You need to pursue your efforts, actions and consequences free of the debilitating fear of failure, and with complete commitment to the team's pictures of success.

Yes, leadership is all this, and more:

- Leadership is always active, never passive.
- Leadership is doing the hard yards to genuinely understand your operating environment in fine detail. But decision-making is the art of making decisions when there is insufficient information, because, as Winston Churchill once memorably remarked, there never can be sufficient information. In short, back yourself.

- Leadership is always decisive. When a decision looks like it may be wrong, a good leader simply summons up willpower and makes another decision.
- All great leadership is about leading yourself as well. All leadership is *personal* leadership. Leadership can be lonely, frightening, confusing, and damned hard work. You need to equip yourself with the skills to survive.
- Leadership is not a title or a status. It is the expression of a purpose.
- Leadership is demonstrated intelligence.
- Leadership is effective communication.
- Leadership is creating an environment in which everyone feels valued.
- Leadership is being passionate and courageous, even if you momentarily feel overwhelmed or afraid.
- Leadership is recognising your limitations and surrounding yourself with people who have strengths in the areas in which you are weak.
- Leadership is being comfortable with who you are. It's authenticity merged with learned aptitude.

If the attributes above sound terrifyingly unlike you, then one of two things is true.

Either you are not a leader, and you should get out of a leadership position before it drives you nuts and you take your organisation down a blind alley. Or, you are recognising that being a leader takes much more than mere willpower. It takes study, determination, self-awareness, and a refusal to be cowed by the implications of the task.

What they never tell you when they hand you the keys to the executive washroom (remember those days?) is that it is very difficult to *act* the leader. And if you aspire to lead, you must learn how.

There's a lot at stake. Unless you are authentic, clear about your vision, values and purpose, and genuinely passionate about what you do every day, it is unlikely that you will have the resilience to succeed through the hardship and setbacks of sustained leadership. The day you feel you're going through the motions is the day you should stop going through the motions.

This may seem like a huge task to take on. It is.

So here is one really simple answer to the requirements of leadership. In fact, if you achieve this, you will have greater control of your team and your decision-making choices every day. And you can achieve this right now.

Be clear about, and **passionate** about, your organisation's driving vision. Not as it is written on some corporate statement, but at a much deeper level. As it affects everything you do and say and work towards.

You can't fake it 'til you make it. Get with the programme, or get out. Better still, drive the programme.

So come on. Be clear: what *are* you working towards?

All businesses start with an idea. A big idea. A grand vision. A moment of insight.

The cliché of the business plan that's initially jotted on the back of a serviette over a long lunch is true for me and many of my clients.

Yet beyond the opportunity of doing what you love and getting paid for it every day, the core vision during the early days of a start up, a new division, a new ... anything, really — the BHAG for the venture, and all the things necessary to achieve to make it happen — can often be hazy at best.

So far (and of course it's early days!) I have been involved in seven businesses from start-up phase as an owner or Board member. Some were successful and some weren't.

If I boil down to the 'why' behind the not-so-successful ventures (otherwise known as dismal failures that kept me awake night after night), it was always **clarity** that was lacking. Clarity about the core vision and about the roles, responsibilities and, most importantly, the expectations I had of my colleagues, both top down, and side to side.

Additionally, I have had the privilege of being part of hundreds of businesses as an executive coach. And this has reinforced my enthusiasm for getting the core message right.

The message needs to be simple, clear, (yes, there's that word again), potent and something that others talk about.

I was chatting to the Stephen Yolland one day as he helped me shape this book. 'What do you think of my business?' I asked. Stephen looked at me.

'What do you hate, Soozey?'

I admit I was confronted. I asked him what he meant. I didn't feel strongly enough to *hate*, I assured him fervently.

He sighed. 'It's a mental shortcut,' he explained patiently. 'We always talk about what we want to achieve, but in my experience it's necessary to know what we hate to really *crystallise* our vision.'

I looked blankly at him. He spoke quietly. 'Alexander Fleming hated children dying of treatable infections. So he invented antibiotics, the most dramatic change in the human condition in history.'

He stared at the ceiling, pondering. 'Martin Luther King gave his energy, his genius, and ultimately his life, not because he hated the white man, but because he hated racism. Hated it with every ounce of his being. We still have not seen the final results of the example he gave us.'

'Fred Hollows hated people being blind because they couldn't pay for a $5 operation.'

I went home and had a good think.

I hate businesses that operate without a vision that engages their staff.

So before we go any further, and keeping it as simple as possible, let me explain the differences between vision, purpose, mission and values.

Your *vision* is what, if you try, you can actually *see* before you. It's the painted picture held in your head, your heart — in your soul, if you like — of where you are heading.

Your *purpose* is the *reason* for the vision existing.

For example, Samsung's vision is to 'Inspire the World, Create the Future.'

Its purpose is to devote talent and technology to creating superior products and services that contribute to a better global society.

Your *mission* is what you want to achieve — it's the actions you take along the way. Samsung places innovation at the core of how it works on projects, to ensure that its products are genuinely revolutionary, so that the change they create is revolutionary, too.

Your *values* are the 'how' you act as you work towards your vision. Ethically. Practically.

I'm guessing that, although it might be a little blurry, you *do* have a vision right now.

You, your staff, your clients, your key stakeholders may get it, or they may not.

So your ultimate vision must be supported by an engaging mission message that fuels your momentum. Something that really lights you up. Something that's new to your clients. Something that really *communicates*.

Is it? Does it?

Is it engaging?

Or do you actually look — internally and externally — like all the other businesses in your industry?

Using Facebook as an example:

Facebook's vision is that people use Facebook to stay connected with friends and family, to discover what's going on in the world, and to share and express what matters to them.

Facebook's mission is to give people the power to share and by doing so make the whole world more open and connected.

This vision and mission makes Facebook so much more than just a social website.

Some more examples?

Nike — Our mission: To bring inspiration and innovation to every athlete in the world.

Starbucks — Our mission: To inspire and nurture the human spirit one person, one cup and one neighborhood at a time.

(And you thought they just sold coffee.)

If your vision is the ultimate picture of success, then your mission needs to exude your spirit, your purpose, your reason for being in business. It must be of value to a wide audience, showing empathy for the world beyond simply 'doing business'.

Your mission needs to create a *shift* in your thinking and the thinking of those who you engage with.

Your mission should be powerful enough to make your competitors irrelevant!

And when your staff shares both the vision and the mission, they share its value in their own way. It's therefore important that you share that vision with them with clarity and enthusiasm.

A clear, compelling vision and mission is good. A *shared* vision and mission is electric!

Your market is only as good as your core messages supporting your vision. The right core messages will attract new staff, clients and raise your profile in the marketplace.

The one constant — the differentiating quality — of a successful organisation is *always* an executive team that provides the necessary leadership. This team has a clear strategy. This team translates and tailors that strategy to market circumstances. This team's enthusiasm as it engages with internal and external audiences means the strategy is communicated in a natural, infectious way.

Chasm closers

1. Where is your business right now? What would you like to achieve for yourself and for the business over the next ten years? Work back from that ten-year point.
2. Answer the 10 questions on pages 60 and 61. Determine your BHAG(s) and align your vision with action.
3. Understand the differences between vision, mission, purpose, values and strategy. Get them clear in your head.
4. Do you have a message to communicate your BHAG, and the strategy supporting it? Is it the right message?
   If you do, your business should be performing better and better. If you don't and you don't address it, you'll continue to work long and hard but perhaps ineffectively.
5. How are you delivering the message for your strategy? The vision? The mission? Charismatically? Clearly? Do people understand it? De-fluff your strategy and the way you share it.

6. Can your colleagues and your staff translate your message into practical day-to-day actions in their job role?

7. Regularly review and re-review your current strategy with your leadership team and ask — often — the following question: based on what we've achieved, what else might we do to enhance our likelihood of success?

8. Constantly challenge your strategy with the immensely powerful question: '*So what?*'

9. Give your staff regular opportunities to have a voice — and give them feedback on their ideas.

10. Strategy is owned by everyone. Who owns it in your organisation?

11. It's important to regularly remind yourself that strategy is NOT planning. Keep it simple!

12. Strategy is never cast in stone. It requires constant nurturing. Do you really get that?

There is one strategy for a given business — not a set of strategies. It is one integrated set of choices: what is our winning aspiration; where will we play; how will we win; what capabilities need to be in place; and what management systems must be instituted?
—**Roger Martin,** *Playing to Win: How Strategy Really Works*

Obstacle 3: Execution

A bird's-eye view of the chasm

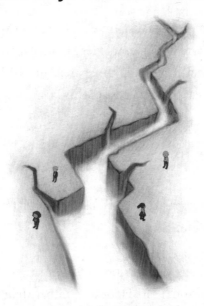

The gap between strategy and execution has always been vague. Much has been written about how to devise a strategy; much less exists about how to implement it effectively.

That's why big consulting firms make significant revenues writing business strategy documents for their clients and then arguing that the strategy will fail unless those consulting firms project manage the strategy implementation.

Academics put together models for communicating the strategy. However, very few of them have earned their stripes in the field actually implementing a strategy with real thinking, living, breathing, emotional people.

Countless books have been written on the topic of strategy and execution. How many of them have ever made a real difference in the real world? Precious few.

Why am I so cynical? Because time and again I can walk into an organisation and ask an employee — often a talented, senior employee — 'What are the top three areas in which your role makes a difference to the success of this business?' and they look at me blankly.

Why?

Because the S word hasn't been *translated* to that person in a way that's meaningful for them.

They are simply there doing a job — to a greater or lesser degree of success and personal satisfaction — rather than making a real difference to the future success of the organisation. (And thus to their own success.)

As a frustrated customer in urgent need of a product or service, have you ever thought of a better, more efficient way for that product or service to be delivered to you? When you have come across poor customer service attitudes, is it not sometimes obvious how tiny changes could make all the difference?

Well, employees know what's wrong, too. When working with teams one of the questions I love to ask is 'If you were the CEO of the business for the next two weeks, what would you change in the business, and why?'

The suggestions invariably stream forth, and they are always around principles of clarity, efficiency, and simple solutions to problems that never seem to get dealt with.

In my experience, people nearly always have an answer and yet often they don't provide their feedback and observations to their managers or the executive team.

Why is it so? Generally because they don't feel that they have the power to do so, or they haven't been *told* that they have. Or they have been marginalised so often that they have lost their self-confidence.

Or worse, they fear being victimised or sidelined if they upset the status quo.

When it comes to process improvement, the view from the top of the chasm provides a real (and rare) opportunity for innovation. All it takes is a leader with the time, interest and insight to have a *real* conversation with subordinates, customers and peers as part of the process.

And a *real* conversation of course, is defined as being 'both ways': talking *and* listening.

Because you know what?

You can start to close any chasm by asking a few key questions.

As a leader, you are supposed to have clarity, vision and purpose, right?

So, challenge yourself: Is there a more efficient or more productive way of getting your strategy implemented?

Yes. Almost certainly, yes.

All *you* have to do is to work out what questions to ask and determine a process that empowers every member of staff to speak out, take a stand and add value — and I mean across *every* area of the business. Consider these very intelligent comments:

To understand execution, you have to keep three key points in mind:

> *Execution is a discipline, and integral to strategy.*
> *Execution is the major job of the business leader.*
> *Execution must be a core element of an organisation's culture.*
> —**Larry Bossidy & Ram Charan,** *Execution*[*]

AND

> *Building a visionary company requires 1% vision and 99% alignment. When you have superb alignment, a visitor could drop in from outer space and infer your vision from the operations and activities of the company without ever reading it on paper or meeting a single senior executive.*
> —**James C Collins and Jerry I. Porras,** 'Building Your Company's Vision'[*]

I agree wholeheartedly: execution is key to strategy, and as a result of excellent execution your vision and mission should shine out from your organisation without the need for it to be articulated in any other way than the behaviour of your people. Can you honestly — *honestly* — say that this is the case? If it isn't, you have work to do. Right now.

Success habits are the key to successful execution

In order to achieve the personal excellence that translates to successful execution, each individual, from you down to the most unassuming people you employ, needs to develop what I call success habits.

Success habits are those regular behaviours and actions that are not only in line with organisational and personal values but which also leverage the individual's innate desires, capabilities and talents.

They vary from individual to individual, but they always have a common theme: it is all about stopping doing whatever holds one back from one's goals, and doing more of what helps to achieve them.

And if it was as easy as just saying it, then everyone would do it.

We need to observe how top athletes practice the same skills over and over again until they develop 'muscle memory' — then their bodies do what is expected of them automatically in times of great opportunity or stress.

Soccer is a wonderful metaphor for team success. I take my sixteen year old daughter to soccer training. Her team just won their championship, and good on them! I really enjoy soccer, but coming from an Aussie Rules country, I know many of my fellow

Australians can't understand why people so love the round ball game, when a single goal in ninety minutes can separate the sides and their passionate supporters. A goal can take a few seconds to score, and for the rest of the ninety minutes it's a dour struggle played out all over the pitch. So why do I often use it as a metaphor for team success?

Consider these words from my daughter:

> *The role of goalkeeper looks like the hardest, loneliest, toughest job on the soccer field. But I love it because it has taught me how to react to failure, how to be resilient, how to rise to a challenge, how to take control of the defensive area, to use my words in times of pressure, how to make decisions with very little time and most importantly how to communicate with the rest of the team.*
>
> *I'm naturally quite reserved, and I have been upset many times over the years because of the 'one' goal that changed the results of our day.*
>
> *I train twelve hours a week, every week: nerves, bloody knees, aching limbs, balancing schoolwork, and yet the measure of success can be defined by just one goal, either for our team or our competition.*
>
> *Playing in goals allows me to see the game, and the ball, being played out from one end of the field to the other.*
>
> *For a goal to be scored, every team member relies on each other. It's the time spent training, managing the schoolwork*

and soccer balance, it's the choice of whether to turn up to training when it's pouring rain, dark and very cold. The goal scored relies on a commitment from every player which includes the obvious skills and abilities, but also courage, focus, and the right mindset and attitude.

So, as the ball is played from one end to the other I can see the years of dedication and commitment played out in every movement of the ball (from both sides) whether it's a footwork trick to put off a defender or the speed and confidence of a committed striker as they run for the ball.

As the ball moves away from me, beyond mid field, I feel my heart rate increase — every time. Often, the ball may be turned around and start heading towards me again, but as it moves toward goal I am so focused. My twelve hours a week and years of training become just one heart-stopping moment.

When we score it's thousands of hours and incredible teamwork that really creates the goal. Even when we defend, it's the same. The spotlight often shines on the striker who scores the goal, but real success begins from the first kick on the field and the hours of training and commitment leading up to it, by every player. We've all got different jobs which allow us to work as a team and create opportunities to win.

No matter how many goals, or how few, every player on the pitch contributes to the success — or otherwise — of the team.

If any one of them goes 'out to lunch' during the game, it's likely their team will lose. And the same is so true of businesses and government organisations. It's all about how the weakest link sees their role in the overall strategy. If they're 'out to lunch', so is your strategy!

As a leader, it's your job to facilitate your staff in developing the behavioural skills they need to operate in the same way as top athletes, but in business terms. You can devolve the implementation of your communications, but leading those communications — ensuring you have clarity and are insisting on that clarity being communicated successfully — comes down to you.

Your people knowing and trusting what they should be doing, and how to do it, depends entirely on the leadership you give and the training with which you back up that leadership. It is not impossibly complicated, but it *does* require discipline, planning and knowledge.

The problem comes, more often than not, with a failure in implementation rather than a lack of desire. After all, if we look around the landscape of human resources practice worldwide, we are constantly encouraging our people to 'set goals', 'aim high', and 'shoot for the moon'.

Yet while we actively encourage their participation in considering our — and their — goals, we very often fail to equip employees with the skill or knowledge that they need to actually achieve them.

Because an unachieved goal invariably causes de-motivation, it would frankly be better, in some cases, not to engage in the process at all.

But by concentrating on critical success habits as well as ensuring that your agreed goals are well understood, you have the chance to embed the behaviours that make goal setting successful in practical and measurable ways.

The alternative is stark: the whole thing becomes a 'once off' verbal and intellectual exercise that leaves employees feeling something of a failure, stressed, de-motivated, and cynical.

Believe me, the prize is worth the effort. In addition to your business benefiting, the transformative effect of real-life success in goal setting encourages employees to *continue* to develop their skills.

So your ultimate aim as the leader is to ensure that the momentum created will be maintained so that the business is less reliant on you and your senior executive colleagues. If the whole lot of you were to (God forbid) walk under a bus, your goals are so well understood, by staff who are so well motivated and trained, that the organisation will continue to function — and succeed — seamlessly.

If that happened to your business now, would the transition be seamless? If not, you need to act. Now.

Because all organisations excel when their teams and individuals are committed to a shared vision and values — working to their strengths and realising their potential — it follows that every 1% you can improve, your organisation will be repaid many times over with lower staff turnover, lower staff replacement costs, greater stability, greater staff satisfaction, better client relationships, and greater productivity. Every area of your organisation, including its bottom line, will be substantially and positively impacted.

Just imagine: could you improve everyone by just one per cent? Just one per cent! Your organisation would be transformed!

Imagine being able to flick a switch and realistically expect 1% lower costs, 1% greater turnover, 1% more profit margin, 1% lower staff costs, 1% more stability, 1% less industrial disputation, 1% happier clients, 1% more market share ...

Because of its universal applicability to staff of all types, from the very bottom of the tree to the very top, this book is one of the switches you can flick and expect to see this type of transformation. With a little help from you and your fellow leaders of course. Plus a bit of elbow grease. A bit of self respect. And a bit of determination.

Determining the size of the chasm

To examine the size of the chasm between organisational strategy and individual activity, which determines the success of execution, you could start by asking your staff a few questions. And also by making sure you keep 'WIIFM' front and centre in your mind.

Wait. What? WIIFM? I haven't been able to find the original source of the phrase *'What's In It For Me?' or* WIIFM. But it's predominantly used by creative people in the advertising industry to keep their audience in mind when they are working out how to brand and sell a product or service.

By continually asking 'What's in it for me?' (by which they mean, of course, not themselves, but the ultimate customer) they make sure they are communicating their sales messages as *consumer benefits*, not mere *features* of a product or service.

Really successful advertising agencies reject creative idea after idea if they don't communicate a solid, demonstrable consumer benefit — the WIIFM — no matter how much fun the idea may be.

An inspiring, engaging leader considers the WIIFM every step of the way: 'What's in it for my people?'; 'How will they respond to this idea personally?'

They ask it when developing organisational goals right through the internal presentations and communications used to explain them to staff, and then onward into the sales and marketing process wrapped around those internal actions.

If you can't determine the WIIFM, you simply can't sell your goals, objectives, products, services, strategies and ideas to others, or help them to define and clarify their own.

Remember human nature: people do things for *their* reasons, not yours!

Make it personal. Because it is.

No matter how good the support structures and systems are that are in place, success in life is always determined by the breadth and commitment of an individual's thinking and then how well they can translate that thinking into action.

That's why your objective as a leader is to ensure that you know what drives your 'direct reports' — and that *they* know what drives *their* direct reports — and so on down the line.

In taking a genuine interest in others (and I mean in *all* aspects of their lives, and not just what you can get out of them), you can assist them with defining that gap between where they are and where they want to be with clarity, passion, and a measurable approach, certain that all potential obstacles and conflicts have been accounted for and accommodated in advance.

So, in a nutshell:

- To be successful in anything you need to be able to recognise a gap or a challenge and come up with a solution. And then, execute.
- But to execute successfully, you need to understand the WIIFM for everyone involved so that they *all* come along for the ride.
- Remember you are only as strong as your weakest link. And remember above all that your weakest link may be someone you rarely personally speak to — a credit controller, a delivery guy, a cleaner, a receptionist. They are not a weak link because of their own roles or actions, but because of poor management.

C A S E   S T U D Y

Jeremy was twenty-one years old, bored at university, and decided to start up his own technology business. He was focused, determined, clear and incredibly fast. In fact, the ongoing challenge for Jeremy was to slow down long enough to listen to his slower-paced team, customers and suppliers.

By the time Jeremy and I met each other, his business was two years old and already turning over more than $1 million per month. He had been really successful in hiring the right staff and getting the right structure in place but he wanted the business to grow faster.

From the outset, I was surprised that someone on the fast track to phenomenal success at such a young age would be interested in working with an Executive Coach. When we got down to the details of what it was he wanted to achieve, he said 'I don't think that I need your help [in a coaching capacity] but I want you to work with my staff. I'd like you to help me implement and communicate our five-year plan. I want to know that they love it here — and I mean, every day.'

Jeremy was self-aware enough to understand that his behaviour had chasm-causing potential.

Rather than invest in himself and develop the behavioural flexibility to inspire and motivate the team, (because he recognised his own strengths and weakness, and his own inability to change), he was smart enough to invest in his leadership team (and okay, yes, a little in himself, too) so that they were clear about their daily activities and completely in line with *both* his strategy and their WIIFM.

He gave them full responsibility for their actions, and had regular 'huddle meetings' so that everyone was across all areas of the business, including financials, and the personal motivation factors for getting excited about their envisioned future, asking them lots of questions about how they related to the strategy he was trying to drive. How did it *affect* them? Them *personally*?

One year later, Jeremy's monthly revenue had doubled.

And the side benefit? Jeremy's company became an 'awesome' place to work too!

So the next time you are trying hard to persuade and influence your key stakeholders *stop*! Think!

The effort that you're making is most likely because of *your* needs, not *theirs*.

Start your WIIFM focus and your BHAG will get closer day by day.

Innovation through GOSPA

It is vital to have a clear destination, but it's also vital to create the roadmap for how to get there.

It is not enough to know that each journey begins with a single step. Your staff need to know what the second step is, and the third, and the fourth …

So, for example, the goal set by the executive team and communicated to the Board may be to increase revenues by twenty-five per cent year on year while maintaining existing profit margins.

I have worked for many businesses with these types of goals and believe me, it's all gobbledygook to the majority of staff outside of the top team or the finance department.

The most successful businesses that I work with go about the execution process in a totally different way: *by asking their staff.*

CASE STUDY

Elizabeth was the CEO of a small professional services firm of sixty-three staff across two offices.

Revenues had hit a wall during the last two years. Elizabeth was working more than sixty hours a week, and most weekends, trying to turn the business around.

The first thing that I asked Elizabeth to share with me was the vision for her business. She was engaged, enthused and clear about what she wanted to achieve and yet most of her direct reports said that she was so stressed and reactive that she actually caused a lot of confusion, tension and feelings of being overwhelmed amongst the staff.

So right off the bat I asked Elizabeth to share her vision with the staff and then leave me with them for a day to determine the gaps.

Every staff member was excited about Elizabeth's presentation and all said that they felt they could play a significant role in achieving that vision over the next three years.

What we discussed was the answers to the following questions: What lights you up about the vision? What do you see as the challenges? What would it mean to you if the vision came true? What contribution can you personally make?

To the last question, we added some structure in determining the critical areas in which each function made a difference to the business across finance, marketing, service delivery, sales, recruitment and products.

From there, we discussed individual goals and objectives.

And, needless to say, the business pushed through the stagnant revenues and back into profit in the following quarter.

Remember: not only is it vital to have a clear goal, but it is essential for you and your people to understand the various stages of the 'road map' to get you there, and to feel they are contributing to the outcome. And that road map is walked one day at a time.

I have been using GOSPA for breaking goals into measurable daily actions since 1994. I'm getting better at it each day. This book is partly my effort to share this excellent structure with a wider audience.

What on earth is GOSPA? It stands for Goals, Objectives, Strategies, Plans and Activities. Here's a snapshot:

Goals

To be successful you need to work hard on the things that matter, the key steps to achieving your ten-year BHAG.

Writing down step-by-step goals helps you to define what's important. And your goals always need to be SMART:

- Specific
- Measurable
- Attainable
- Realistic
- Time-bounded

Goals must be of *importance* to you. The attainment of a goal must fulfil a fundamental need for you and your organisation. And in attempting to attain them, you also need to be able to answer the great six questions of Rudyard Kipling's 'six honest serving men'.

I keep six honest serving-men
(They taught me all I knew);
Their names are What and Why and When
And How and Where and Who.)
—**Rudyard Kipling,** *The Elephant's Child*

Always be clear: goals are an 'end' in themselves, not a 'means'. They are the answer to 'What?' They are *achieved* by How, When, Who and so on. It breaks down like this:

1. WHAT do I want to achieve (Goal)?
2. WHY do I want to achieve it?
3. WHEN do I want to achieve it by?
4. HOW will I achieve it?
5. WHERE will I achieve it, or WHERE will I find the resources I need?
6. WHO do I need to assist me?

Last but not least, Goals must always be in line with your values. Because those are not negotiable.

Objectives

Objectives are the means to the end. They are the How.

They quantify the milestones on the way to the goal.

They can be negotiable. They can change: subtly, or substantially.

You can lose a battle and still win the war!

Strategies

Strategies outline your long term options to achieve your objectives.

They are ideas. They are creative. They are imaginative.

Failure, more often than we realise, is the result of our own failure of imagination.

They begin to detail required actions in broad brushstroke terms.

Strategies focus on the immediate challenges to forward momentum, but they may take a long time to play out in full.

Plans

Plans prepare for the action.

They prioritise time, and focus.

Plans list everything needed to achieve the objectives.

They describe the course of the action and the 'must do' activities.

Plans eliminate distractions and irrelevant activities. They allow you to discard unnecessary or distracting activities, to 'sacrifice' them to the bigger goals.

Plans prepare and organise the necessary resources and capabilities.

Activities

Activities are the specific things you do to achieve your plans.

The quality of and commitment to the activities determine ultimate success.

At this level, behaviour has the greatest impact.

You can go to the book website for a GOSPA planning sheet at www.iamtheproblem.com.au. It's free, and we welcome you knowing more about it.

So how do you know whether you're planning to deliver on the 'right' priorities?

Go back to your BHAG and over-riding strategy and then integrate your teams' responses by working through GOSPA with each individual according to prioritised responsibilities. You can do this personally or devolve it, but it is a process that is the key to success so don't give it to someone you don't think will give it due weight.

Consider this:

The key to innovation is allowing people to take risks and giving them the time for reflection and debate. Abraham Lincoln once said, with great perception of the difference between success and failure, 'If I had eight hours to chop down a tree, I'd spend six sharpening my axe.'

I reckon Abraham Lincoln and GOSPA fit together hand-in-glove!

The Top 9 Tips

As you work through GOSPA, use the 'Top 9' tips.

1. Clarify the Goal as it relates to delivering the BHAG. How is achieving your Goal going to make the big picture happen faster, more thoroughly, and more successfully?

2. Break the work up into projects with clear, measurable, achievable outcomes, milestones and delivery dates. Don't be frightened if this results in a multiplicity of little projects. It always does. And decide in what order they need to be done. Then, if you end up with an 'implementation gap' — that's to say the difference between what you *set out* to do, and what you *actually* do — at least you will have done the most important things.

3. Create one 'owner' for each project *and* each activity. This isn't necessarily going to be the manager. There may be other people in the team that can take on the role and better manage timeframes, deliverables and resourcing requirements. So this can also be seen as an opportunity to develop individuals.

4. This is an opportunity for creating a leadership culture that extends beyond you and your immediate reports. Preferably these people will be permanent employees of the business so that you retain the experience, lessons learned and give your existing staff the opportunity to learn and grow. Only use external consultants as you absolutely have to, and use them to train your people, not replace them.

5. Ensure that the team or organisation's purpose is clear and agreed by all people delivering the work. And that they're clear about how their personal work impacts on the over-arching strategy.

97

It's worth repeating: nothing succeeds like clarity. Repeat the BHAG often, and test whether your teams really believe in it. If they don't, retrace your steps, and re-engineer until they do.

6. Required outcomes at each stage need to be clearly documented. If there is an implementation gap happening, don't bury your head in the sand. It's to your advantage to know sooner rather than later that some targets will be missed or delayed.

7. Ensure that any external stakeholders involved in delivering the work are clear about the importance of the commitments made around time and deliverables. Share the bigger picture purpose with them. If they don't step up to the mark, bite the bullet and replace them.

8. In the event of a variation to the plan, make sure that people are told early, openly and that a new schedule is discussed and agreed with all key stakeholders. When it comes to change, over-communication is the best remedy. Never leave anyone overlooked or uninvolved.

9. Clearly articulate and communicate the risks involved in change, including unsettling your people. For many people, change is scary. Discuss strategies for risk mitigation as a team. Write them down, and re-examine them on a regular, pre-planned basis. Situations change. This can alter your risk profile. Check it regularly and encourage your people to speak up if they have any concerns.

CASE STUDY

A specialist manufacturer was having some repetitive challenges with a particular make of container.

The problems seemed to be intermittent and challenging to fix. Over the prior eighteen months the estimated cost to the business was $750,000. Now, that's hard costs.

As I chatted with their CEO he articulated a number of other unmeasured costs such as down-time, customer frustration, brand damage and at least one customer moving some of their manufacturing work to a competitor.

During a coaching workshop with the team, it was the office manager who talked most about this concern.

Hardly surprising: she was the one who often took the complaint call from the customer and co-ordinated container returns and resource management.

The following day, she made up a huge professional-looking sign and installed it on the workshop floor entitled 'Zero Defects!' The sign had a number of milestone dates for the twelve months ahead.

Here's the email that she sent out to all workshop staff:

By now you will have noticed our new sign on the shop floor.

Starting immediately, we are aiming for Zero Defects coming out of our factory.

I will update you at our team meeting each month on how we're going.

In the meantime, the little red arrow will move up the sign every Friday if we have no returns.

If the arrow keeps going up for the whole month, we will be celebrating with pizzas, beer and some entertainment that will knock your socks off.

If we last for the whole quarter, I'm planning a huge event for you and your families which includes jumping castles, face-painting and pony rides.

I'm already booking the entertainment for the event so please, please do all that you can to make sure that we achieve our goal. (Otherwise the boss is going to kill me because there's a cancellation fee!)

I am putting together a revised risk plan. If you have any ideas to share that will improve our chances of achieving Zero Defects, please let me know.

How's *that* for initiative? How's *that* for leadership?

Within three weeks, the otherwise complicated defect was fixed. Unfortunately, there was a return of *another* product the following month but they eventually had their party!

Using the Top 9 tips as guiding principles for your workplace will not only improve processes, it will give every staff member the opportunity to lead.

And what's that worth? Trust me: it's priceless! It sends out a message that everyone is a leader regardless of their title or position. *Everyone.*

CASE STUDY

I began working with a client very recently who is just into his third month of SMART goals and using GOSPA.

The firm is a niche, specialist organisation and my customer is the divisional manager of the Professional Services team. When we first started working together, he was reluctant to discuss the specifics around his KPIs because he manages a time-and-materials team who are reliant on sales from other divisions.

Kicking and screaming, we commenced this quarter with SMART goals with KPIs written by *each team member themselves*. The financial target averaged $20K per consultant per month (averaged across the business) and we had a business plan and individual GOSPAs to give these targets some real meat.

Yesterday, we sat down and he took me through the targets against actuals and here are the results:

Month 1:   His team exceeded their target by 1.9% during what is usually their quietest month of the year.

Month 2:   They exceeded target by 34.2%.

Month three is already looking good. Based on these results, we were initially concerned that we were way off with our targets.

Although we believe in our processes, it all seemed too good to be true. So, we did some research to find out the average billings per consultant per month and per year for the previous twelve months. The result? Assuming that this trend continues the way that it has started, there will be an increase of seven per cent per consultant for the year.

Now do the math for your business. What would that sort of result be worth?

This is the key point to understand.

Goals, objectives, strategies and plans are all future-focused but they give us clarity, direction and improved communication with our peers, staff and subordinates from Day One. And shared, measurable goals develop passion and innovation in a team by increasing engagement levels. Individuals begin to see their roles through a different lens.

We can measure the daily activities that align to those goals and communicate those activities in a way that has meaning for the business.

So: review your goals, objectives and KPIs during the coming week and ask yourself the following questions:

- Do I believe that we can achieve this? *Really* believe it?
- Have I discussed my KPIs and communicated them in a way that's meaningful to my team? Have their KPIs been set with their active involvement?

- How do I best communicate our success on a daily and weekly basis?
- How are my actuals tracking against target?

Once you've answered these questions and tweaked your KPIs, discuss them with your leaders. If you find you have any challenges turning intangibles into tangibles, agree on what you need to do *as a team.*

The danger of 'training' and how it often leads us astray

No matter how smart its systems or IP, an organisation can only be successful if its people are committed, fulfilled, and aligned with the organisation's goals.

To get to this exciting place, some training systems seek to take external skills and 'graft' them onto the employees, like new branches onto a tree.

But in the pressure of the real world many such grafts fail — they are not given ongoing care to ensure the grafted skills are developed and honed, to properly incorporate the branches into the living organism of the tree.

Sometimes there's a training budget per person and individuals often choose how that discretionary money is spent. And that's good empowerment, to be sure. But, of course, self assessment of one's training needs is not always correct.

For example, I have noticed that in the majority of technology businesses that I work with, most of the technicians do not choose any 'soft skills' development (as they call it) as part of their annual training. Instead, they prefer to further invest in technical skills training. They perceive this as more important for their personal success and advancement. Explaining that this isn't necessarily the case is an important step towards creating more vibrant, worthwhile teams.

For this reason (and a few others) I am skeptical about both the motivations for, and the implementation of, 'training'. Yes, of course, it's a necessary part of growing the skill set of individuals and organisations. But 'having a training program' is often used as an excuse for not developing people in fundamental, life-changing ways that are in tune with your strategic goals.

If you have a specific customer service problem, for example, you may train the customer-facing people in your organisation to make sure they don't mess up, and that customers walk away satisfied. All well and good, and honourable. And possibly profitable. But it may — just may — prevent you from examining the deeper strategic issue that caused them to have to deal with customer concerns in the first place. See what I mean?

In fact, I often think about how strange the whole HR-cum-training system in large corporations really is. HR are usually a part of corporate services and HR in particular has a significant role to play in determining salary packaging, training, job scopes and measures, performance management and overall engagement for service delivery, but mainly for staff with whom they rarely work, in job roles that they have never personally experienced. That's a recipe for poor management.

(Excuse my cynicism. I know that it's not like this all of the time but I see it often. Way too often.)

So, one of the biggest challenges for business is in getting this whole system to align.

As I keep saying, that's all about mapping roles and responsibilities to organisational strategy, and aligning individual goals and objectives to the team goals and objectives.

Please understand: I'm not talking here only about job descriptions and KPIs. I'm talking about aligning individual intent to organisational vision.

I'm talking about *involving* your staff (not just directing them) and aligning their skills development with those areas that will help individuals to better achieve their goals and execute your strategy.

Oh, and for *them* to pro-actively measure their success along the way.

So who is ultimately responsible for this required turnaround?

Well, it's the CEO and each of the divisional heads isn't it? And now we have come full circle.

As I mentioned earlier, the CEO can sometimes have the loneliest job in the business. And, to make matters worse, the corporate-style structure that most businesses adopt makes it even harder for the CEO to measure individual success, in a way that's meaningful and engaging for *every* member of staff, let alone measure corporate success on an accurate and ongoing basis.

That's why to me the most significant role of anyone in leadership is to help others understand and work to their strengths, producing easier and measurable growth for themselves and their organisations. It's all about showing them how to consistently make the most of who they are.

The word 'consistently' isn't just thrown in there for good measure. It is role- and outcome-crucial.

Person by person, habit by habit

We have a sign in our office. It's to remind us what we are helping our clients with. It reads: Changing Thought is Good, Changing *Actions* is Great.

I don't think anyone can argue with that logic.

As a leader, your focus needs to be on always creating positive, active and ongoing change in line with the growth of the organisation, person by person, habit by habit.

No-one approaches each day with a completely fresh slate. We all develop habits in our personal and professional lives. Some of these habits will contribute to our success, and others are inhibitors. We will talk more about it later.

Likewise, no single individual, no matter how successful already, has a perfect 'basket' of actions and processes. No matter how long we have been doing our job, we can all improve.

After all, in our professional lives we quickly learn that the smartest people aren't always the most successful, nor are successful people necessarily the smartest.

The real success stories are always those people who 'just do it' more consistently and more often than everyone else.

And organisations that are full of such people are always the most successful in town.

As Jack Welch famously said: 'Strategy is simple — just pick a general direction and execute like hell!'

This is always — always, always, always — true

I repeat: this is not rocket science, but it *is* fundamental.

1. The starting point for positive change is in each individual understanding how they're perceived, understanding what their strengths and limitations are, and how their actions will impact positively or negatively on the core organisational strategic compass.
2. Most importantly, that they understand those areas of performance that need focused, timely attention as they work towards achieving greater and greater results for their teams, clients and the organisation.

3. And then, that they see the adjustments necessary as satisfying their own needs, individually, as well as the organisation's needs.

Most organisations have some grasp of 1 and 2. It's when they get to 3 that their mind goes collectively blank.

Part way through a recent change program an apprehensive VP asked me 'How do we know if the teams and individuals understand the new strategic focus for the business? How do we know that they really get it? What's my litmus test to see if they're on track? That they're really buying in?'

Good question.

Sometimes simple behavioural observation can tell you. This is what it looks like when they 'get it'.

- They are self motivated
- They embrace and adapt to change
- They welcome and measure individual and team success
- They celebrate successes together
- They take risks, and learn from mistakes
- They foster learning and growth
- Engagement is high
- Individuals and teams have robust conversations in line with business growth
- Innovation is common

All of this can be measured!

What if they *don't* get it? What does *that* look like?

- They resist change and you will hear some whinging and moaning up to the highest levels in the business
- They focus on the job and the tasks only
- They hide from you, and from assessment — so measuring individual success becomes harder to achieve
- Staff turnover increases
- Engagement levels are low
- They are reluctant to have robust conversations
- The culture is reactive, fire-fighting and staff get caught up in 'busy-ness'
- There is a risk-adverse culture and innovation is rare

All of *this* can be measured too.

Interested in measuring these things? Design your *own* culture survey. It's not like there aren't a heap of good ones out there to look at for ideas. Involve your staff and give them a voice in envisioning your future. Involve them in everything from your vision, mission, BHAG, goals and KPIs. Measure — confidentially and courageously — whether they 'get it'.

If you don't think they 'get it', but you're not sure how to design and implement the survey yourself, then employ one of the better 'corporate alignment' firms around and get them to do the work for you. They can point you in the right direction: it'll be money well spent.

Is this sounding risky? Scary?

Hey: if the CEO of IBM could ask more than 319,000 global IBMers to participate in redefining their values, maybe you could do it too. What's the real risk? Finding out something that's uncomfortable?

You have to be courageous. You. Before anyone else will be.

In their ageless book *First, Break All the Rules: What the World's Greatest Managers Do Differently*˙ Marcus Buckingham and Curt Coffman offer a myriad of ideas to improve employee satisfaction, engagement and great work culture. The book analyses the results of 80,000 interviews with managers conducted by the Gallup Organisation over a twenty-five year period.

One of the biggest themes in the book is that the top leaders treat *every* staff member as an individual, helping to create an environment where they can work to their strengths and celebrate success. I know that this sounds like common sense, but my career demonstrates that few leaders take the time to do this.

Oh, and a quick and dirty paragraph on Performance Management

Please, please, please remove the language of *performance management* from your vocabulary, from your meetings and from your dialogue.

Performance management is just a component of a much bigger picture and, used on its own, it often makes the rest of the picture hard to see.

Start talking about *performance alignment*. Start taking *top down responsibility* for the business and where it's heading in a way that's meaningful for everyone. It's up to you to help your people to see, feel and hear themselves making a contribution to something much greater than they ever realised.

Something about *them*, and their hopes, not just about you and yours.

Performance management is often a Band-Aid fix. While bad apples are as perennial as the sun, poor performance is rarely the fault of the individual.

By the time an HR conversation is required it's often too little, too late.

Performance needs to be a regular, timely conversation — in the moment, and in line with strategy. OK, end of rant!

So: are you genuinely interested in developing a culture of personal engagement and responsibility instead of mere accountability?

Performance *alignment* is the way to do it top down.

Chasm closers

1. Make your BHAG visible in some way — a wall plaque,
    a sign, the intranet, what you say at meetings, whether
    internal — or, if appropriate — externally. (If you have a
    great BHAG, it'll probably get out anyway — where's the
    real danger in carolling it far and wide from the rooftops?
    You may find people want to help.)

    In short: keep your BHAG alive in every conversation.
2. Get your team together and discuss your vision. Talk about
    what you're working towards over the next three to five
    years. Ask for their feedback and ideas.
3. Ask the key questions: What lights you up about the vision?
    What do you see as the challenges? What contribution can you
    make? What difference will it make to you? Yes, you personally.
4. Explain GOSPA and all have a go at completing your own
    GOSPAs top down. You will be surprised by the results!
    Make sure you don't mix up all the different parts — be
    clear about them.

5. Once everyone has completed their GOSPAs, the most difficult work is actually done. Now, document your GOs (Goals and Objectives) into a one-pager and diarise your activities on a daily basis.
6. Keep your Gs and Os close at all times.
7. Review your G and Os last thing at night and first thing in the morning.
8. Prioritise your Activities in your diary in line with your GOs every day. Make sure everyone else does, too.
9. Keep the language of the SMART goals and GOSPA alive and growing throughout your leadership team, and encourage them to demand the same from their reports. Keep talking it until it becomes second nature.
10. Do a culture survey — who gets it? Who doesn't get it? Why? Or, use a professional provider to do the survey for you.

Look for the positive — and create your own luck

So, that's just put the world to rights, huh? It's all dead easy.

Er, no.

You may encounter inhibitors along the way to achieving your strategic goals and objectives. As with so much in life, PERSISTENCE is key.

Many great goals have been set but it is those few people who *remain optimistic* and *persist* through challenging times who achieve truly outstanding results. They are perceived by everyone else as the lucky ones, of course!

I well remember South African golfer Gary Player's pithy response to the commentator who told him, after a fine round, that he 'had been lucky today.'

'Funny, that,' said Player, 'the more I practice, the luckier I get.'

I make no apology for repeating the much-quoted aphorism on persistence from American President Calvin Coolidge. It is, in my opinion, one of the wisest and most significant things ever said about the human condition.

> *Nothing in the world can take the place of Persistence.*
> *Talent will not; nothing is more common than unsuccessful*
> *men with talent. Genius will not; unrewarded genius is*
> *almost a proverb. Education will not; the world is full of*
> *educated derelicts. Persistence and determination alone are*
> *omnipotent.*
> *The slogan 'Press On' has solved and always will solve the*
> *problems of the human race.*
> **—Calvin Coolidge**

Obstacle 4: Culture

A bird's-eye view of the chasm

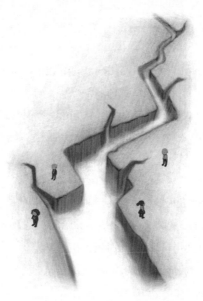

On one side of the chasm the executive team are waiting on the results of the next culture survey, hoping that there will be an increase in engagement levels from last year's survey.

The executive team knows that the Board is using the survey results as one of the measures to determine the overall performance of the business — and they're sweating.

'Have I implemented the changes that will make this place a great place to work? Why are the retention numbers about the same as they were last year? Why haven't HR made this more of a priority?'

On the other side of the chasm the staff have taken precious time to respond to another survey. Shaking their heads as they click on the boxes … 'Why does the exec team bother with this? I did this a year ago and nothing's changed. Just a serious waste of time and money. Apart from my performance review last July, this is the only contact that I've had from HR. Nothing will change.'

Why bother?

Sound familiar? Interestingly, the chasm closer is simple.

You need to provide timely feedback, share a plan, determine the actions that you're going to take and decide how you'll measure success.

You're going to involve every member of staff. You'll give them the opportunity to have a voice. That's what the culture survey is for, after all. But, you know all that, right?

So, why doesn't this happen?

Well, I'm going to stick my neck out and say that one of the biggest challenges in the corporate sector — and of course it's no secret — is that the CEO's performance is rewarded on the short-term financial goals of the business.

Where's the incentive to plan long term? To create a winning culture? Both are all too easily sacrificed to the clamour of short term demands.

So how do we define culture? And is it really important? As important as other stuff like productivity, profit, and so on?

Many CEOs and senior managers misunderstand culture. They think it's all 'lovey-dovey-touchy-feely' stuff that isn't 'hard management'. If they do anything about it, it's way down the list of priorities, or it's done begrudgingly as an afterthought.

This is because they lack one basic piece of understanding.

Survey after survey reveals that culture *determines* productivity, profit, and so on.

A great internal culture is not a 'nice to have', it's a *must* have.

And if you think about it for a moment, it's so easy to create a culture! All you have to do is bring people together and give them a little time, and perhaps a little gentle guidance.

Human beings are innately co-operative animals. Our natural instinct is to work together. Don't think about wars and conflict. They are generally the result of poor planning, poor leadership, and inadequate 'systems' of consultation.

Think instead about the vast humanitarian outpouring when there is a natural disaster. Think about philanthropy. Think about communal pride. Think about tribes. Think about the relentless pace of industrial, scientific and social change, driven by co-operative effort, century after century.

Bring people together and in no time they will be interacting with each other, responding to their environment and forming processes and behavioural patterns that are sometimes conscious, sometimes not.

As an organisation grows, new people join and adapt to the culture. As the years pass, some of the original staff may move on but the *culture* remains. That's what culture *is*. It's not a 'top down' diktat. It's thousands of things — every minute of every day. It's in the way we say 'good morning.' It's in our posture, our eye-contact. It's in the way we answer the phone and respond to problems. It's in the way that we recruit and induct new members to the team. It's in the way that we take responsibility and *choose to turn up.*

It is the expression of who we are *together.*

The right culture can be electrifying, motivating and the basis for efficient, highly successful businesses. Sadly, the wrong culture can also be toxic and erode the confidence and effectiveness of otherwise happy, motivated people.

It's easy to undervalue the importance of culture. As a line manager in a multi-national said to me recently, 'What's the good in having a great culture when we're not profitable? At the moment profitability is my primary focus.'

I understand this thinking but I also know that if you concentrate on building a great culture, you WILL be more profitable, as sure as day follows night.

A great culture can make the difference between turning a profit and making another loss. Culture affects retention, recruitment,

innovation, brand, productivity, sales revenues and profit —
positively, or negatively.

So, instead of trying to nail custard to the plate, let's see if we can
drill down. What exactly *is* culture?

Culture is a combination of:

- ethics
- values
- behaviours
- visions
- systems
- dialogue
- myths
- stories
- language
- attitudes
- environment
- habits
- beliefs

Ignore any of those things, and you'll do half a job. When you
leave one of those areas untended, weeds grow.

So, yes, culture is a combination of all the 'fluffy stuff' which (by
the way) can be measured and re-measured to gauge your progress.

But although it's fluffy stuff, culture translates directly to people's
attitudes and actions. It's a shared way of working passionately
towards something tangible.

The better the culture, the less procedures and processes a company requires.

So culture turns up on your bottom line.

How do you create a *great* culture?

Great cultures are created and nurtured by great leaders.

So here is one really simple thing you can do to improve your leadership of your organisation.

In fact, if you achieve this, you will have greater control of your team and your decision choices, every day!

Be clear on — and passionate about — your company's vision and values.

That stuff again huh? Yes, you'll find it's a recurring theme. Again and again, it reveals itself as vitally important to closing chasms of all kinds. If you achieve this, at the very least, then those around you will take up the cudgels on your behalf. They will be 'lifters not leaners'. Their enthusiasm becomes self-sustaining, because you have provided clear, passionate goals for them to aim at.

General Patton, widely regarded as the most charismatic and effective attack general of the American Army during WW2, said, 'Leadership is the ability to get things done through others for their reasons.'

I'll continue to pound one point home: one differentiating quality of a successful organisation is *always* a Chief Executive Officer with a clear vision and values. A leader who is grounded in the present, but who also clearly articulates where the organisation is going and how it is going to get there.

Most importantly, they have the skills to inspire, motivate and excite others when they talk about their vision, so that their vision also becomes the vision of many others.

In time, other leaders rise and take ownership of the vision as their own. These people are the custodians of the culture. And without them, no company can continue to prosper.

So, how do you go about maximizing the effectiveness of your fellow leaders and direct reports in order for you to achieve the vision?

1. Be clear about the vision and *why* it's important to you and the business. Keep it simple.
2. Share the vision formally, regularly, and informally.
3. Inspire your direct reports to share the vision.
4. Know your direct reports' personal motivations for achieving the vision.
5. Make sure they *really* believe it. If they don't truly share the vision as if it is their own you're in trouble because, the moment your back is turned, it will fall in a heap. So question them closely and listen to their answers.

Simply, it's about focus: You must consistently employ all five of these actions.

Last but not least

This is utterly vital: the CEO has to be *present*! And I don't mean sitting at the desk on their computer.

They need to be hands-on with the workers. Regularly. You cannot inspire by being invisible, or just a face on a newsletter.

Get out of your office, and often. Be seen. And be seen to listen.

CASE STUDY

One of the most successful start-up organisations that I have worked with in Australia built their business up from nothing to $18 million in revenue in just three years.

The vision was clear from the start: to dominate their chosen market.

From the beginning, the business's values were evident to us in every dealing we had with them. The business fairly *crackled* with values that were embedded into their very fabric, from recruitment and induction through to performance alignment.

It wasn't about what was written in their brochures or on their website. You could see the vision and values of the organisation at a behavioural level when interacting with their staff.

The CEO was very clear about what he was out to achieve and surrounded himself with people who had strengths in the areas in which he needed the most support.

He was clear about his priorities and spent most of his day supporting his direct reports and helping them to support him effectively to achieve the company's vision.

Each member of the leadership team were clear about their financial targets and they were all extremely hardworking but, then again, they also partied hard — and together, of course!

In other words, they made hard work fun.

From the outset, I never saw myself as a 'supplier' or 'service provider' and I was never seen as one by the client. In fact, at a Christmas party, the CEO introduced me to *his* client as one of the team. He said, 'Soozey does all the things about my job that I can't do or don't have time to do.'

I was very proud of that endorsement.

And yes, I see my role as a partner who ensures that my client achieves their mission.

Of course, I am also a culture custodian for every one of my clients too.

Some just 'get it' faster than others!

Delivering to the vision

If the vision is clear, you communicate it regularly with enthusiasm, you understand your direct reports' personal motivation factors, and you've checked that they are telling you the truth when they say they share your vision, then how do you make them accountable to *delivering* it? Well, (as you might expect by now), that is also up to you!

Here are some effective and easy-to-implement tips for success.

The vision and mission aren't just etched into the glass

I have worked with organisations that have spent millions of dollars on their logo, branding, communications and strategy and yet when you ask about their vision and values they have to check the website, the etched glass in the foyer or the inside back cover of their latest brochure.

A mission statement is a lot more than a form of words. It needs to have personal value. It needs to give every member of staff personal purpose. If it's not simple and clear, change it. And then start talking about it, and 'living' it!

You can't accelerate without the 'right' passengers on the bus

Recruitment is one of the trickiest tasks in any business. And yet, it's often done under pressure with little or no thought about the impact of a bad choice. When the pressure is on, we are often very optimistic about the candidate sitting in front of us because of their resume, their reputation and the likelihood of them doing a great job for the business.

The most important roles in the business are the leadership roles. These people have an impact on the culture before they've even opened their mouths! The cost of a recruitment mistake at this level can be hundreds of thousands of dollars in reduced productivity and disruption — and very often within a month or two (not that we would ever add up the cost of course).

So, how do you mitigate the risk? Well, the first step is to breathe deeply and *take your time*. Take your time to ensure that the job description, performance measures, structure and expectations for the role are all in place. Take your time to run all of this information past the other members of the leadership team. Take your time to ensure that a formal recruitment process is in place including a way of measuring the candidate's skills and experience against the Key Selection Criteria.

Is this starting to sound too heavily administrative to you? Are you questioning whether or not you have the time to put this much effort into finding the 'right' candidate? If the answer is yes, then put all of this effort into finding and partnering with an Executive Search firm that will assist you in mitigating the risk. Don't hesitate.

Your ability to build high performing teams around you is paramount to the business's success. One of the most important relationships you can develop is with Executive Search Partners that understand you, your business, your industry, your strategy, and — critically — your personal values and the critical elements you look for in your Executives. Start building these relationships NOW if you haven't already!

'Too expensive?' do I hear you say? I understand we all need to keep an eye on the bottom line. But what's the cost of a recruitment mistake? Interestingly, while we can always pull out the invoice from an Executive Search company and whinge about how much they charged, the cost of a recruitment failure isn't something that gets measured very often. There are the hard costs such as salary and time — they're the easy measures. And, then there are the costs of losing staff engagement, lost opportunities for new business, deteriorating client relationships leading to lower revenues and so on. Do Executive Search appointees ever go wrong? Of course they do, but you have (or you should have) a guarantee in place so you can go back to them and ask for another option. All of this makes a placement fee for an Executive Search partner a brilliant investment.

I could write another book on just this topic. It's something that I'm passionate about because I'm so often called into businesses to 'fix' the people problems that should never have started in the first place — at the recruitment phase! It really boils down to people who just don't fit the culture. For me, being outside of a business, it always stands out.

So, instead of another book on the topic, here are Soozey's top tips for getting the passengers on the bus who are the 'right' fit to accelerate your business:

1. Take the time to write a job description that includes the business strategy, goals, values, success measures, the Key Selection Criteria and personal attributes required. For a sample template go to www.iamtheproblem.com.au.
2. Run the job description by all the peers who will be working with your new team member. Involve them in the process and ask for assistance. Finding a new team member is a team effort — or it should be. Ask 'What are the top three areas in which we will measure the success of this role?' The answers to this question will help you in refining the Key Selection Criteria.

3. Determine a process for measuring the success of each application against all of the measures above. Each task can be measured according to skills, alibility, knowledge and behaviour.
4. Work with an Executive Search partner to find a pool of applicants weighted against your criteria.
5. Get other members of the team involved in interviewing the shortlisted candidates
6. Beyond the interview, ask the shortlisted candidates to make a presentation in a specific area that is pertinent to their success in the role.
7. Use a behavioural tool (at least one) between final interview and reference-checking. The behavioural tool will assist you with your reference-checking questions. By the way, if you think that reference-checking is a waste of time, it is if you ask standard, general or closed questions! Put some time into preparing your questions. It's amazing what you hear when you listen — really listen — to the answers. Of course, your Search Partner can always do these and give you a report.

Remember, the interview is often the best that you will ever see of this person! So if you have any uncertainty at all, don't hire them.

Be there for them

Minimise your number of direct reports and make sure that the majority of your conversations align to your mission. There is a direct relationship between the effectiveness of your direct reports and the time that you make available to them. According to a recent article in CIO magazine, no less than four per cent of your annual work year — or 9 out of 230 days — should be spent with each direct report, and that's the minimum.

Get personal

Ask why they think they are being paid — what are they working towards? What or where do they want to be in two years or five years?

Don't be offended if they think they will have moved on, even to another company or organisation. (The idea of a cradle-to-grave 'one company' person is hopelessly antiquated. People now have three or four *careers* in their life, let alone three or four employers. So that's perfectly acceptable if that is their goal today: false and overblown 'loyalty' is a highly destructive thing.)

And don't be offended if they have ambition. One of our clients — a CEO — asked a twenty-five year old with high potential where he wanted to be in five years. The answer was, 'Don't get nervous, but I see myself doing your job in five years.' The CEO was delighted: indeed, the most charismatic leaders recognise that their protégés must, inevitably, succeed them one day. Unless you want to work forever?

Work together to create a five-year development plan. What skills, behaviours, attitudes need to change in order to get there? What support must you provide to help your key people to get there? This will help you with your succession planning and along the way your team productivity will soar!

Frame the goals intelligently

Use every possible opportunity to reinforce the bigger picture of what the team and the business is working towards, in a way that's meaningful for your audience.

There are many 'things' in life that give us bursts of happiness, but lasting happiness is built on meeting three human psychological needs. They are:

- Belonging — connecting to others and feeling a part of something bigger then ourselves
- Competence — taking on challenges and contributing in a way that makes a difference in the world
- Autonomy — wanting to do things that reflect our personal values

Research has shown that when setting goals, you (and your team members) will fall short of lasting fulfillment if you are not satisfying at least one of these three basic needs.

Interestingly, the way in which we measure success within organisations is about financials, individual performance measures and activity-based results. All of these things give us short-term highs resulting in common comments such as 'You're only as good as your last sale,' or 'We've won that deal, let's plan for the next.'

To focus on things that provide lasting happiness and the stickiness that creates great cultures, focus on establishing goals aligned to both your business vision and the three critical psychological needs: Belonging, Competence and Autonomy.

We should talk about them a little more.

Belonging

One of my clients is an IT recruitment business.

In a one-day team meeting, every individual in the business shared their goals and objectives in line with the business strategy.

They also shared their personal goals, what they needed from the team, what inspired and motivated them and what it meant to come to work every day.

Most importantly, each business unit shared the story about how they were going to celebrate success upon the achievement of their goals.

The following Monday, one of the team members booked the venue where they would be celebrating their successes twelve months later — without asking for permission first. The team member 'Belonged'.

Competence

One of my favourite client stories this year has been with an advertising firm.

The Administration Manager made an off-the-cuff remark to me one day about nobody taking much interest in adhering to process.

When I asked her about the business benefits of everyone getting their timesheets in on time and completing the business case paperwork thoroughly, her eyes lit up. We then went through a process which measured the *financial* benefits of the administration team to the business.

Suddenly, the mindset of the administration team went from being the 'process naggers' to 'success measurers.' They were so proud of now being understood as a key part of the business's profitability and that without them doing their job competently, the business suffered.

How much better do you think her team became at 'selling' the benefits of good internal reporting to everyone else?

Autonomy

Sarah spends every holiday volunteering in orphanages in third world countries.

She is studying social work part-time and has a full time office management role.

From the moment we started conversing about the way in which Sarah's role made a difference to the organisation, she began talking about her 'one day' social work career. So we digressed for thirty minutes and explored how her future career could align to what she's doing right here, right now.

Sarah became the ambassador for national fundraising activities across the whole business, raising support for AIDS orphans in South Africa. Sarah organised fun runs, bike rides and social activities, and the CEO agreed to match every dollar raised with a dollar from the business.

Who do you think became the biggest culture custodian? More importantly, what effect do you think this undertaking had on the culture?

Frame the goals differently

Yes, you may have a financial goal to increase your revenues by twenty-five per cent year on year. Yes, you may want to increase your client spend by ten per cent and your profits by three per cent but do these numbers ignite individuals? Not likely!

Frame the goals differently. Allow each member of staff to have a voice. Think innovatively, and translate the goals into the language of autonomy, competence and belonging.

Thinking in these terms might be the best use of time you ever make.

Expect that mistakes will be made

Yes, you read that correctly!

In her book *Mindset: The New Psychology of Success** Carol Dweck talks about the power of the word YET.

When starting something new, give yourself — and allow others — the OK to make mistakes.

Language such as 'I don't expect that you will be great at this straight away. I understand that it's going to take time and that you will make mistakes along the way' gives people the crucial permission to find great solutions because they know they can mess up and not get fired.

Interestingly, the psychological research behind this shows that if you create a culture where people are allowed to make mistakes, it actually lessens the likelihood of mistakes happening.

Being scared of error and worrying about what others think all the time actually undermines performance.

It's OK if you don't know all the answers right away. It's OK to call upon others for help, or simply use these three special words yourself sometimes: 'I don't know.'

Create a culture of less error — and increase creativity as a side benefit — simply by saying that it's OK to make mistakes.

Feedback

Provide feedback regularly. Very regularly.

Don't wait for some hugely formal annual review. Arrange quarterly meetings and track people's progress against the two and five year plans.

Also, chat informally as often as you can. Regularly tap into their personal motivations for being at work. Personal questions such as, 'How is the Paris holiday planning going?' are much more motivating than 'Why are we five per cent behind target for the month?

Give honest, regular, timely and accurate feedback.

Without losing authenticity, consider people's feelings. Praise — with purpose — in public. Always correct and provide constructive feedback in private.

Remember the golden rule about corrective criticism. Create safety for your direct report to acknowledge the correction as a positive, creative moment. The simplest way to do this is to remember 'PCP': Praise — then correct — then praise again.

This is not wishy-washy sugar-coating of the pill. It is common sense and courtesy.

(By the way, if you genuinely can't think of anything to praise your staff member about, you have a bigger problem to solve.)

And in any interaction, don't forget to ask for feedback on *your* performance too! Give people permission to tell you the truth.

Actively deal with poor performance

Don't be afraid to bite the bullet and correct poor performance.

A twelve-month study, released at the Australian Conference on Culture and Leadership in Sydney 2004, surveyed more than one thousand Australian organisations. A staggering sixty-three per cent of workers reported that their managers took little or no corrective action when someone was under-performing. This made the performing workers bitter and sapped their confidence.

In short: the under-performer feels deserted, and the performers around him or her feel that they are unfairly carrying a burden. Everyone loses, including your organisation!

Think BIG and stay there

It's very easy to micro-manage when things get out of hand. Resist the temptation!

You very often don't need to know the detail. You only need to know when a decision affects the business.

Have confidence in the communication systems you have in place and the people you've chosen to support you.

Only intervene if you see *weakness* in those systems or people, or if you genuinely believe you are the *only* person with the skills or knowledge to fix the situation.

And what does that say about your quality of recruiting and/or training, by the way?

Listen

Encourage your reports to be 'real' with their feedback to you. Jack Welsch, the inspirational former CEO of GE, says that the greatest quality of a leader is to encourage subordinates to 'tell it like it is' and be prepared to follow through with appropriate action.

If more CEOs understood this, and inculcated the idea into their corporate culture, then half the business calamities we read about in the papers simply wouldn't happen.

Delegate and stretch

Challenge them! Give your direct reports challenging assignments that push them outside their current comfort zones. Provide honest feedback. Let them learn from their mistakes. From the words of Helen Keller, remind them that 'life is a daring adventure or it is nothing!'

Resist the temptation or need to always 'be right'

It's one of our basic human drivers to 'be right' because it helps us to make greater sense of the world.

Psychologists call this 'confirmation bias'. It's something that many leaders suffer from and it is the reason behind many business partnerships breaking down. Here are some examples to bring this concept to life for you:

A CEO has it stuck in his head that long hours = dedication. He hires a new head of marketing and thinks that person is doing a wonderful job because he is at his desk from early in the morning and still there 'hard at it' until late in the night.

What the CEO doesn't see — because of his confirmation bias — is that the marketing manager is there long hours because he can't delegate, he is micro-managing to the *nth* degree, and also that he is actually continually being rescued by his team and doing a less than average job himself.

Another example? (And a very common one.) The CEO who has a chronically under-performing Board constantly talks about their strengths because they are 'family' and can be trusted. That CEO is sheltering in the comfort zone of their confirmation bias about what *matters* on a Board.

Another? The CEO whose business is in financial difficulty who constantly talks about their expansion because of his pet project: signing a ten-year lease on an extra 200 m^2 of storage room. Meanwhile revenues — genuine expansion — are collapsing.

Or what about the Head of Sales beating his chest about famous successes from years gone by but neglecting to acknowledge or learn from his recent mistakes?

Confirmation bias is something that isn't conscious. At a deep level, we *need* to reinforce information that reinforces our decisions — *whether they be right or wrong.*

And that's how our beliefs become our self-fulfilling prophecy, for good or ill.

There have been some catastrophic global financial decisions in recent years which are a testament to this idea. So, try, try, try to be open to the challenge that confirmation bias creates.

Am I saying that you should believe in nothing? Absolutely not.

Just be *mindful.* Be open to the dialogue that you're hearing. Don't isolate yourself. Don't assume that 'only you know'. Test your dearly-held assumptions in the fire of others' opinions.

Yes, sometimes what you're hearing may not be worth listening to.

But sometimes, there may be pearls of wisdom if you linger in the game of doubt for just a little longer.

Who knows — you may even make a different choice or take a different course of action.

It's not about doubting yourself. It's about being rational. Remind yourself regularly: finding out you were wrong is the best way to 'be right'.

Provide opportunities for development

Reward employees with interesting conferences, coaching and training that helps them to achieve their career goals.

For example we have a client at a mid-size professional services firm who has her sights set on a brass plaque outside her office that says 'Partner'.

In order to receive a promotion next year, she has to raise her profile. So the MD has invested in a presentation skills coach to assist her in confidence-building for conference and key note presentations.

Sure, she might be a high potential Generation Y, full of fashionable, world-weary cynicism, but how highly do you think she now speaks of her organisation? She's just become another culture custodian!

If there is one thing that you can take away from this chapter, give some thought as to what actions will improve your ability to inspire others in your team, your division, your organisation, your circle of influence and your community. And always remember this wise advice:

> *Tell me, I forget. Show me, I remember. Involve me,*
> *I understand.*
> —**Carl Orff**

Spread the values

The majority of businesses that I work with have a set of values.

Interestingly, these values on their own are usually nothing very exciting.

For example, many businesses boast similar values such as integrity, trust, commitment, courage, innovation. But these are essentially motherhood statements. And if they *weren't* your values, by the way, then what are you doing in business or public life at all?

In the end, it's not the values themselves that make the difference; it's the story behind the values and the interpretation of the values through every conversation. It's the values *in action* that count.

So what *are* values and what do they mean to your organisation's success?

- Values are timeless.
- Values bring the behaviours of a business to life.
- Values have intrinsic value.
- Values define us: who we are and what we stand for. They are our guiding principles. Our compass.
- Values don't change.

Samuel Palmisano joined IBM as a salesman in 1973 and was promoted to CEO in 2002.

In 2003, Samuel invited more than 319,000 global IBM employees to participate in redefining the values of the business for the first time since the company was founded.

It was conducted via the global intranet and branded the 72-hour 'Values Jam'.

Here are the IBM values statements that resulted:

- **Dedication** to every client's success
- **Innovation** that matters, for our company and for the world
- **Trust** and personal responsibility in all relationships

Clearly, leading by values is very different from some kinds of leadership demonstrated in the past by business. It is empowering, and I think that's much healthier. Rather than burden our people with excessive controls, we are trusting them to make decisions and to act based on values — values that they themselves shaped.
—Samuel J Palmisano, Chairman, President and Chief Executive Officer, IBM, 2002-2012

Listen: if IBM can manage an exercise like this with 319,000 IBMers, you can manage it in your own organisation.

So how do you ensure — how do you *guarantee* — that your staff share the core values of the organisation?

Sorry: you can't and you won't. However, you can recruit to your values and facilitate the opportunity for your staff to participate in a process that gives them a voice.

Here are some tips which my clients use:

Give all your staff a 'say'

Arrange a date to get individual teams together. Make it regular. Here is an example of a recent email sent out to all staff in a professional services firm ahead of one such meeting:

> *Our firm is successful because of everyone's contribution and hard work. We have grown quickly over the past four years and we want to ensure that as we grow we retain our unique culture. It is very important for every successful firm to have a vision and to be able to articulate our values — as these underpin our culture.*
>
> *It is also important to be able to express your personal objectives and goals, with the aim of making sure your personal objectives and career objectives can be aligned.*
>
> *I look forward to your participation in the coming workshops.*

In preparation for each team session, prepare everyone with some questions to get them *thinking* about the values, behaviours and attitudes that are important to them.

It's really important that participants are not put on the spot; that they are given a week or so to think through the questions below and articulate those values that are intrinsically important to *them*. Here are some example questions:

1. Who am I in this organisation? What do I do? And how does what I do fit into the 'big picture' of the business?
2. What do I want to achieve at work?
3. Why is this important to me?

4. What is it that I enjoy most about coming to work every day?
5. What do I choose to tolerate at work?
6. What can I do to positively change my response to what I only tolerate?
7. What do I enjoy most about my role?
8. What am I looking forward to in the business?
9. What are the stories that are told about the business?
10. What impact does our behaviour have on the culture?
11. What or who inspires me most at work — and why?
12. What is it that I do that makes a *real difference to the culture?*
13. How do I *measure* success in my role?
14. What are my personal goals? How does the company fit into *my* bigger picture? Why is this important?
15. What are my core values? Why are these values important to me?
16. How do others see my values in action?
17. What happens when I have a values conflict? How do I respond physically and emotionally?

Let your staff know that they will not have to share the answers to these questions with their colleagues unless they choose to.

This questionnaire is for your and their eyes only! Encourage them to be utterly frank, and if they don't know the answer to something, to answer 'I don't know.'

During your session together break everyone into groups and get them talking about the vision, mission and values: beyond what's on your brochure or etched into the glass at reception.

A great opening question is 'Where do you see the business in five years' time?'

If they get stuck, be more specific with 'How many staff? Where will our offices be? Will we be national, international? What markets will we be active in? How many Partners or Senior Managers? What sort of clients? What will be the same? What will be different? Products? Services? Innovation?' Etcetera.

From there you can start to drill down to the values that are important and the behaviours that bring the values to life using the answers to the questions above as a starting point. Ask them:

- What values are important to you as we work towards our future vision?
- Why are these values important to you?

This exercise alone will create the opportunity for all your staff to have a voice in the direction of the business and to tell you what's important to them.

During a recent workshop of this kind one of the influencers in the group said 'Wow, I hadn't considered myself being here in five years. After today, I do want to be here and I do want to make a difference in the culture of the firm as we grow.'

That workshop alone locked in this one enthusiastic employee for the long term, and in doing so reduced recruitment costs, reduced knowledge loss, reduced training costs, and reduced the implementation lag that always occurs when one employee leaves and another takes their role. A bargain, don't you think?

What do our values look like in action?

The next stage is to discuss the *behaviours* that bring your business values to life.

- How are we going to keep these values front of mind in every interaction?
- How do we make these values part of our dialogue, our narrative, our internal and external communication?
- The leadership team are the most important part of this process. How are they going to hold each other to account?

From there, you can start to write a values statement for each value.

What's the 'right' number of values?

The majority of businesses that I work with end up with 3-5 core values that are infused into every aspect of the organisation. Here's a great example from Hewlett-Packard:

Trust and respect for individuals

We work together to create a culture of inclusion built on trust, respect and dignity for all.

Achievement and contribution

We strive for excellence in all we do; each person's contribution is critical to our success.

Results through teamwork

We effectively collaborate, always looking for more efficient ways to serve our customers.

Meaningful innovation

We are the technology company that invents the useful and the significant.

Uncompromising integrity

We are open, honest and direct in our dealings.

Above all, never forget: Culture happens!

Remember: regardless of whether you choose to impact your culture, it will happen — for better or worse.

Pro-actively *choosing* to influence your culture in alignment with your core values and vision can ignite a workforce if it's done right.

Chasm closers

1. Live your vision — always. And all ways.
2. Survey your staff and determine those areas that need your primary focus to improve the stickiness within your business.
3. Communicate the results of the survey to your staff. Note: *not* communicating the results will reduce engagement levels!
4. Tell your staff about the actions that you are going to take to address the results of the survey. Keep them posted. Over-communicate.
5. Communicate openly about how the business is tracking — and share the financial results!
6. Develop a values communication plan and incorporate your values dialogue into every aspect of your business
7. Journal your answers to your chasm closing questions below and invest some time and thinking to your own values and behaviours — and the impact that *you* individually have on the business.

Chasm closing questions for you

- Is my vision clear?
- Do I communicate my vision and values on a regular basis?
- Do I communicate my vision with enthusiasm and clarity?
- Does my behaviour align to our values?
- Do I tap into my direct report's personal motivations for achieving the vision?
- Do we have the structure and processes in place to keep the vision and values alive?

If you don't have the answers, then ask your direct reports, other members of your team, your clients, and your vendors.

The most successful, productive, profitable businesses that I work with *live* their values, vision, mission and behaviours. They give a lot of thought, time and energy to administer processes that make the vision part of the very fabric of their communication — top down.

Culture happens. Whether you plan it, or not. And culture affects your bottom line.

Obstacle 5: Energy + Mindset

A bird's-eye view of the chasm

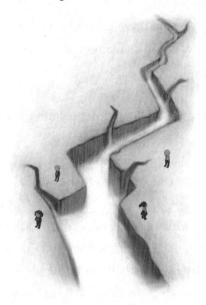

Here's the thing.

Your thinking rules your energy levels, and your energy levels determine your experiences.

Energy *follows* thought, not the other way round.

Think about that.

The way in which you *choose* to respond to your environment — and you choose by how you think about it — determines the way you'll spend your time. It determines how you build and expend your energy. It also determines your level of happiness.

So let's have a look at our chasm. On one side we have the leader who believes he has a clear vision, is driven, results oriented, determined, focused and clear.

The reality though is that these are his best intentions, but he gets caught up in the goals and challenges of his peers, subordinates, and colleagues.

His inner dialogue is actually self-deprecating as he labours over the P&L.

He works long hours and struggles to get to any non-work events.

At night, work keeps him awake and, as much as he tries the well-worn route of journaling his actions and managing his ever-increasing 'to do' list, he is actually suffering in silence, on the edge of the chasm. He perceives the chasm but isn't sure what to do about it, so he just keeps on keeping on. In reality, he is burning out.

On the other side of the chasm are the employees who really admire their leader. They enjoy riding in the wake of the businesses success with their captain at the helm.

They are aware of the fact that the business has hit a revenue snag over the last couple of years with revenues about the same amount as before but with a two per cent decline in profit. But they're not sure exactly why: everyone in the business puts it down to the economy, oh, and that acquisition that didn't transition as well as we would have hoped. But because the CEO tries to be upbeat, no one knows the CEO is desperate and rapidly drowning.

Does this sound like a cliché? Well, yes it is. Sadly it has become a cliché because it's all too common. I see it almost every week of my working life in one form or another.

I have a theory as to why this occurs. And I put it down to one thing — ***thinking***.

Blinkered thinking. Routine thinking. Fixed thinking. Leading to treadmill behaviour. Hoping like hope that the problems will get fixed, not realising that it is his very outlook which is *causing* the behaviour which is *leading* him inevitably down the wrong path.

Let's jump back a stage.

Why do most people start businesses? It's usually because they were really great at something, saw an opportunity in the market and started out on their own. But the little (and critical) secret that a lot of entrepreneurs don't share is this:

Even if you're the most brilliant technician in your niche, it doesn't make you a successful entrepreneur or business leader.

Business leadership, management, and entrepreneurship is something that needs to be learned, and not through doing an MBA or a Director's course but through *experience.*

And, that experience is usually 'practicing' on your clients, your subordinates, your peers and colleagues! With varied outcomes.

So, how do you speed up entrepreneurial learning? How do we make 'being the boss' easier?

Plan.

Plan, plan, plan, plan and then plan some more.

Inspirational US football coach Vince Lombardi said it beautifully: 'Plan your work, and work your Plan.'

I don't mean stare at the ceiling endlessly. And I don't mean point in one direction and keep going no matter what, either.

Plans are active. They are pro-active. They are responsive. They are revised. They change as our experiences evolve us and our organisation. They are a living thing.

The challenge in running an organisation is to *keep* plans *conscious* and keep them *active.*

Then, as if that wasn't hard enough, we have to make this 'conscious' planning part of the fabric of our internal and external communications too.

The biggest challenge in any large organisation is that it's up to the perennially busy leadership team to ensure that planning happens, and that it's duly communicated and aligned to strategy.

So what difference does 'conscious planning' make?

I have seen some amazing, extraordinary things over the years.

I've seen a business owner previously working an average eighty-hour week instead catch the 5:35 pm train home to his wife and five children, every day.

Planning saved his family, and probably his life.

I have seen a managing partner take his first holiday (no email or mobile communication with the office) since founding his firm many years before.

I have seen a CEO take long service leave of nine weeks to travel the world with his family — and I also saw his business revenues grow in his absence.

I have seen an entrepreneurial CEO write her 'bucket list' and turn her then-broken marriage into a true lifetime partnership. (That was nine years ago and they're still going strong.)

I have seen businesses grow, families reconnect, valuable experiences be had and revenues increase — yes, all at the same time!

That said, I'm not a big believer in the simplistic concepts of 'work-life balance' or 'time management'.

Work and life is not a balancing act nor is time something that we can manage.

The way in which we *choose* to live is an *internal* game. One that we grapple with throughout every day.

It's about self-management, happiness, choices. To me, it's about being conscious about what we *do* with time, rather than just tracking it.

A happy life is about creating space to think, to plan, to envision.

It's about determining and communicating priorities with those who play a significant role in your life.

It's definitely NOT about being one person in the office and another at home.

It's bringing the best of yourself to the table, no matter what you're doing.

Instead of using the terms 'time management' and 'work life balance', I prefer to consider what it is you're working towards and then find and nurture the type of energy that is going to get you there.

Remember: energy follows thought

In 2005, David Foster Wallace gave a commencement address to the graduating class of Kenyon College and shared a wonderful story.

> *There are these two young fish swimming along. An older fish swimming the other way nods at them and says 'Good morning boys. How's the water?' The young fish swim on, and after a while, one says to the other 'What the hell is water?'*

The point of the fish story is merely that the most obvious and important realities are often the ones that are hardest to see and talk about.

It's really easy to forget or not even notice your environment and the bigger picture, and get caught up on the day-to-day reactive behavioural habits of 'being the Boss'.

Be aware that to others, your behaviour and response may seem strange. They may even find it demotivating or worrying. To you, it goes unnoticed — it just *is*.

It's important to remain conscious of the 'water'. In terms of your organisation, the 'water' is made up of the way that you think, respond and duly act.

Why is it important? Because energy follows thought.

That energy could demonstrate itself in your chosen mode of communication, your attitude, your language and the way in which you manage your time, or the time of your colleagues.

Your energy can have an effect on your key stakeholders, your revenues, your clients, your culture. Let's face it, it has an effect (positive or negative) on your overall success.

We all have different likes, interests and good and bad habits that inhibit or sustain our success. So, this chapter is all about better understanding *yourself*, why you *choose* to do what you do and what you can change to make things better.

The reason that I get called into organisations is always specific and usually relates to revenue, profit, stress levels within the leadership team, conflict, retention or culture.

Often, when I meet the executive team, they can't actually put their finger on what the cause is but they can always clearly articulate the symptoms.

One of the first questions that I always ask is 'how does this current situation with the business make you *feel*?' The answers that I get are always similar. I often get responses such as 'frustrated, angry, disappointed, overwhelmed, challenged, desperate ...'

Then I move onto the challenging piece which is to further explore feelings: 'What could be *possible*? If we turned this challenge around, how will you feel then?'

Feelings are not something that are generally explored, discussed or even mentioned in an organisational context (especially male-heavy organisations) so I usually have to sit and breathe in the silence for at least fifteen seconds before I start getting responses.

One of the most wonderful responses that I have received in the last eighteen months was from a very stressed CEO in his mid 30s who said 'I reckon I will live to be over forty and that would be fucking awesome!'

Other responses have included 'being back in control, satisfied, relaxed, happy, content, clear, open, growing, momentum'.

And the most common response? 'Confident.'

All of these words describe a *feeling*. It's not about strategy, priorities and to-do lists. It's about feelings. And to me nothing else *really* matters because our feelings influence our happiness, our behaviour, our language and our environment.

So the next step is to work out how to get *more* of your chosen feelings into your day.

If I use the thirty-five year old CEO as an example, the feeling that he wanted to create was a sense of control. The business had been through phenomenal growth during the two years prior to our meeting. But during our chat, I noticed that his face was flushed, his breathing was shallow, and his communication flighty and distracted.

He used many large, agitated gestures when communicating and I saw beads of perspiration glimmering in his receding hairline.

Clearly, he was under significant stress and he reduced his verbal expression into one word about how he felt. 'Frustrated.' He spat the word out in a mixture of fear and anger.

The business had been founded by his grandfather and successfully run by his father for the last thirty years. Now, the future of the family fortune seemed to be this guy's responsibility. But in reality, *was* it?

This is where our journey began and we discussed the many ways in which he could create greater responsibility across the executive team and the business to lift some of the pressure and responsibility off himself. Needless to say, his executive team duly welcomed the added value and trust shown in them.

So challenge yourself: what about *you*? *How do you feel* about where the organisation is, right now? More importantly, how would you *like* to feel?

What do you think that you need to change in order to get more of that *feeling* in your day?

Being a decision-maker, every day

Success is a CHOICE. And so, nearly always, is failure.

If we are undisciplined in our approach to achieving our goals we often fail at the first hurdle because something — something that is often less important *but appears urgent* — gains precedent over them.

Your ability to solve problems effectively and efficiently determines your success level. Management and, more importantly, self-management, is about being responsive, decisive, creative and flexible — qualities that are tested on a daily basis.

Remember: you are a problem solver, a decision maker. How many decisions do you think you make in a day?

How could you make them better?

We are often challenged and restrained by our problems and decisions because of the *risks* involved in choosing a path to take.

We know that there is never going to be a *guaranteed* right choice but what is the *best* approach and how do we *mitigate our risks?*

One way is to consider the opinions of those around you, but not to be constrained by them.

Napoleon Hill, the hugely successful author of *Think and Grow Rich** — it has currently sold over 70 million copies — describes opinions as the cheapest commodities on earth!

Another (much ruder!) way to describe it is the famous aphorism 'Opinions are like arseholes — everyone has one!'

The most successful people that I have had the privilege of working with over the years have been those who are quicker than the average person to make decisions and who then follow them through with a greater sense of urgency.

Decision-makers have the courage of their own convictions. Without being over-burdened with the opinions of those around them — by asking for them, listening to those opinions, but not slavishly following them as an alternative to making their own mind up — they *persist* with their decision until they have achieved their goal.

As President Harry Truman said (he even put it in a sign on his desk) 'The buck stops here.'

And if, along the way, it becomes clear that they have made a less than optimal choice, they just make another decision: to change their mind!

Taking the right course

You know that there is never going to be a guaranteed choice. But what is the best approach and how do you mitigate the risks and optimise your decision making ability?

Remember that, on average, you make approximately 50,000 decisions each day. Of course, the majority of these are impulsive, unconscious, reactive, habitual, situational decisions that you don't take any time to really think about, most of which don't have a huge effect on anything. But some do, and those can be stressful! Little wonder decision makers can get tired.

Your ability to solve problems effectively and efficiently is a great determinant of your success.

Consciously improving your decision-making ability will make you more effective in managing your time, reduce your stress and make it easier to achieve your goals. Some people make decisions with ease and others can't even decide what to cook for dinner! It is a skill that we can all improve.

Did you know there are companies out there that do nothing but help you make decisions? They are called 'Decision Support' organisations. They use a whole variety of tried and tested techniques to make better decisions, more easily. If you don't know what those techniques are, then you're making your life harder than it needs to be. And that probably means making everyone else's life harder, too.

If you are challenged by a particular decision, use the following ten-step process to make it less stressful to resolve. Bear in mind (as mentioned in the Self Management chapter) that the process of making a major decision depletes your willpower.

Ten step decision-making process

1. Consider your behavioural style.
   Do you need lots of information? Are you a procrastinator? Do you make assumptions? Do you go with your gut feel? Do you have a high or low level of trust? Pinpoint what you could change about your behavioural style to improve your decision-making.
2. Put your problem *in writing.*
   Define it clearly and state the facts. You simply won't find the answer if the problem is not crystal clear.
3. Ask yourself the following questions out loud:
   a. What do I *really* want to achieve? What's the goal?
   b. What am I trying to *avoid*? What do I fear?
   c. What am I trying to *maintain*?
   d. Is this a single problem or a subset of something bigger?
   e. *Who* else is going to play a part in this decision?
   f. Who does this decision affect? How will they respond?
   g. If I fail to solve this problem, what will happen?
   h. When do I need to decide by?
4. Now restate the problem as a *question.*
   Write the question down at the top of a blank piece of paper.
5. Come up with 10 ways to solve your problem!
   You will find that this process helps to reinforce your intuitive ability.

6. Get one or two senior colleagues to do the same thing. Compare their answers to yours.
7. Consolidate and prioritise all of the answers into a single list in line with your goal (the answer you gave for 3a above)

At this point, you may well have made your decision. If not, continue with the following steps.

8. Discuss your top 3 answers with others in your leadership team. Gain feedback and reprioritise.
9. Grab a big sheet of paper, create a table and SWOT the top 3 choices — What are the Strengths, Weaknesses, Opportunities and Threats *for each choice*?
10. *Make a decision!* Go with your gut feel. By using this process, you have considered and mitigated all of your risks.

Mitigate your risk, or at the very least, your perception of your risk, and therefore your stress level, by developing a plan B at the same time — not when the you-know-what has hit the fan.

The more options you have, the more certain you will be that you are in control. You will also have insights that are not necessarily obvious to others because you have engaged your creative mind in making the decision.

Cheer up a bit! If you use the ten-step process to make a major decision, then at least you can relax, because you will probably be right, or at least as right as you could be!

But OK. What if you're not?

Well, put it down to experience!

1. Admit *quickly* that you have made a mistake and move on. Have the ego strength to say 'I'm really sorry, but I've made a mistake.' To yourself and others.
2. Cut your losses. Stop the leakage. Staunch the bloodflow. Find a new source of whatever it is you need: support, money, customer satisfaction.
3. Develop the habit of using Zero Based Thinking. Developed by personal development expert Brian Tracy, Zero Based Thinking is a question that sums up your experience to this point and gives you the option to start over. That is: *Knowing what I know now, if I had the opportunity to go through this all over again, what would I choose to do differently?*
4. Review your goals and/or go to plan B!

The great thing about life is learning. Many of the worries and challenges that you have right now will have started as opportunities at some point. Recapture your enthusiasm by reversing or heading sideways, instead of banging your head against a brick wall. There is never a right time to stop travelling down the 'wrong' road but this process will certainly assist you on your travels. And always remember what author and columnist Dale Dauten once wisely said:

> *Just because we increase the speed of information doesn't mean we can increase the speed of decisions. Pondering, reflecting and ruminating are under-valued skills in our culture.*

Happiness enhancers

Are you aware of the energy depleters and energy enhancers in your life?

It is a fact that the more energy you have, the more positive and effective you will be.

Happiness is a state of mind. Happiness is when your thinking is positive.

So happiness is a choice.

Psychologists agree that you can choose your mood every day — and that includes even people who are suffering from anxiety or depression — by combining at least three of the following happiness enhancers.

Think carefully about the enhancers that work best for YOU. Here are some ideas to create the mood for effectiveness:

1. THINK about the impact of WHAT you're thinking about!

'I think therefore I am' postulated philosopher Rene Descartes in the seventeenth century. In the twentieth century, psychologists have studied how our self-concept (how we think about ourselves) actually becomes our reality.

In short, we become what we think we are. If we think we have a bad memory or lack confidence then we will sub-consciously act in accordance with this thinking to perpetuate this self-fulfilling prophecy. Remember 'confirmation bias'?

But if we change our thinking we can change self-perception and ultimately, our whole life and the life of those around us.

So, change the channel! Actively block negative thinking with the word 'Reset' and then think a positive thought or re-state your otherwise negative thought in a positive way. If you fail at the first attempt, pause. Keep trying. Keep going until you have actively re-framed your negative thinking. Repeat this process a few times whenever you notice your 'sinking thinking' kicking in.

It sounds laboured or clumsy, but 'Reset' works. It is one of the approaches used by Cognitive Behavioural Therapy to assist people in choosing positive thinking outcomes.

2. Ask the questions that will give you a positive answer

We are constantly asking and answering questions in our mind, and even out loud for some of us! Some of those questions are good for our motivation levels and some of them bad: 'Oh, why am I so stupid?'; 'Aren't I fat?'; 'What have I done to deserve this?'; 'Why is life so unfair?' Those don't help.

The trick is to ask the questions that will give you the *positive* answers. Why? Because thoughts create feelings which create your perspective. Which creates your actions.

Your thoughts really do determine your reality, your environment, and your truth. And your energy — what you do with your thoughts — then permeates the environment of yourself and others in a positive, inspiring, motivating way or in a negative, heavy, sinking way. The choice really is yours.

*Think about your goals and ask yourself a positive question before going to sleep and a positive question when you wake up. By doing this, you help to **choose** your mood for the day!*

3. Diet and exercise

It has been clinically proven that twenty minutes of exercise four times a week increases the levels of the vital brain chemical serotonin in depression sufferers. So imagine what it can do for everyone else!

Regular exercise and a well-balanced diet of fruit, vegetables and non-processed foods creates more energy, reduces stress levels and helps you to live longer.

(It has also been shown that eating chocolate does not contribute to your calorific intake if no one sees you do it. Actually, that's not true, that's just what I tell myself.)

Oh yes, and while you're exercising and eating better you should laugh more, too. That also improves your brain function. Yes — it's a scientific fact! Buy a funny DVD. Read jokes on the Internet. Or just *make* yourself laugh. You'll soon find that you start to laugh spontaneously more often!

Drink alcohol in moderation. It doesn't *really* relax you or make things seem simpler. It just postpones dealing with them. As a wise man once said 'I used to drink to down my sorrows. Then one day I woke up and discovered they'd learned how to swim.'

4. Write a 'to do' list

If you are working on your high pay-off activities in order of priority every day, you will feel more in control and have higher energy levels.

5. *Expect* that things are going to be great

If you have a positive expectation, then time and again things *will* go well. The side benefit is that when you come across minor obstacles throughout the day, they won't get you too down in the dumps. A daily list of activities that are in line with your goals will assist you in creating that all-important positive expectancy.

6. Regular distraction

Get out of the office at a reasonable hour at least once a week. Go to a show, play golf, enjoy a favourite meal, spend more time around children, see a great band, walk in a forest or on the sea shore, visit a museum. Do something you've always wanted to do but never made time for, catch up with happy, positive friends, (that one is vital), go to a bookshop or see a movie — all these are instant happiness enhancers!

7. Find a hobby

Do you have an interest that you get so engrossed in that time melts away? Treat yourself to art classes, journaling, or a creative writing course. Participate in volunteer work on a regular basis. (Nothing will enhance your mood and sense of purpose more quickly.) Work with glass. Learn a sport. Educate yourself. Build a model. Sing in a choir.

8. Put a smile on your dial!

Dale Carnegie says 'if you act enthusiastic then you'll be enthusiastic' and, you know what? It's really hard to feel or act low with a smile on your face.

9. Develop the attitude of gratitude

Express your thanks through a handwritten note, an impromptu visit or a phone call. And keep a gratitude file in your email inbox or drawer — the times people have thanked *you*. Every time you need a quick fix happiness enhancer, just go to your 'feel good' file!

Start the day with gratitude. You are alive, with virtually limitless possibilities for every remaining day you have on this earth. So wake up and say thanks. You can't help but be positive if you start like this.

Success is a choice

You are holding in your hands a vehicle to assist you to achieve outstanding, amazing results in your work and personal life, and a huge leap in your personal satisfaction.

But you can never forget this: it doesn't matter how good the content of this book is, it's up to *you* to take the first step on the ladder and to keep climbing. But where do we get the energy and self confidence to keep doing so? Consider this piece of wisdom:

It is not the skills we actually have that determine how we feel but the ones we think we have.
—**Mihaly Csikszentmihalyi,** *Flow: The Psychology of Optimal Experience**

If we *think* we're going to succeed, we are much more likely to actually do so. Start by being aware of all your skills. Do an inventory and remind yourself often!

The most important thing you need to develop

In my estimation, determination — stickability — is the single most important thing you can develop as an individual.

But how to get there? Some days we feel determined while other days it's more difficult, right?

For centuries, philosophers have been exploring what motivates our desire for 'success'.

The first thing we need to ultimately acknowledge, of course, is that 'success' is highly subjective.

We may not be able to define humour, but most of us know when we've heard something funny — because it affects us physically and emotionally: we laugh! In the same way, we know when we have achieved success because it affects us too. We feel happy, peaceful and in control.

In fact, nothing gives us more satisfaction than knowing that we are on the right path to achieving something that is of *personal* importance.

So let us, as a starting point, use the following definition:

Success is contentment with your life's achievements right now.

In other words, success is about achievement on and in *your own terms*. And it is about results rather than intentions.

If you are not content with your achievements you may be aiming for the wrong things, not working hard enough at them, or stymied by lack of a successful process. Reading this book carefully and acting on the advice in it should help you move past any sticking points.

Bear in mind, your likely success will be dramatically improved by planning — we said that earlier — but planning on its own, without concrete actions as a result, can be an energy-sapping, stagnation-inducing trap.

You must actually begin to act upon and achieve clearly identified goals to maintain your energy levels and momentum.

Merely wanting success, even planning for success, is not enough. If you don't create viable, meaningful actions from your planning then any success you gain must be regarded as simple luck, and inside you will know it. You will not build self-esteem and confidence — the happiness that comes from creating a plan that you bring to fruition.

As to deciding on worthwhile personal goals; well, how successful *are* we if we aren't working towards goals that matter to us personally and deeply? Indeed, it could be asked, if we aren't working towards our own goals, whose goals *are* we working towards? These are very uncomfortable questions for some people, especially those in mid-life. Most people avoid them. But if we don't address them, years can pass until a troubling thought — prompted by the road not taken, usually — stops us in our tracks. At best, we can dismiss it and comfort ourselves that everybody feels this way at some time or another. At worst, it can be like grieving the loss of a loved one.

Success is a feeling. And it's progressive, taking time to become apparent. Like a great coffee, instant success just doesn't taste like the real thing.

Glimpses of perfection

Having grown up in the IT industry, I have spent thousands of hours with extremely bright, hardworking, analytical, incredibly talented people. The majority of whom are also, sadly, perfectionists. The problem with perfectionism is that the goal may be to write a book, exhibit at an art exhibition, set up a business — whatever — but years can go by without the big goal, the ultimate goal, being reached. And sometimes, the final goal is *never* reached, for whatever reason.

Does that mean those lives are failures? Are the people unhappy?

Yes, sometimes. Because some of the most talented people on this planet never actually give themselves the opportunity to shine, or be happy. They should be taking huge pleasure in their myriad of successes along the way, but because those successes are not seen as the ultimate goal, they are ignored.

As you can imagine, these are some of the people that I love to work with the most. In the beginning they have some challenges planning their lives (because it has to be 'exactly right') and they have even greater challenges achieving their goals. In the beginning it's fear of making a wrong choice or a mistake. In the end it's the goal of perfect correctness that cripples the process.

If this is you, get this in your head:

There *is* no prize for perfection.

For one thing, your idea of perfection is rarely the same as everyone else's. Brain surgery has to be perfect, or the controls on a moon lander. Very little else, in reality, has to be 'perfect'. Done is better than perfect, almost every time.

'Done is better than perfect.' I wish I could stick that on ten thousand billboards around the world. It would make the planet a much happier place.

The prizes in life are doled out to entrepreneurs — social, communal or business — who start, start, start. And then *keep* going until they start the 'big' thing that's going to give them the greatest reward. Along the way, they make sure they are having a blast in line with their inner needs.

So, to the perfectionists out there, as harsh as this may sound, get *prepared* to put your art out to the world. JUST DO IT! Make a choice. Get a coach. Commit to an outcome. Prepare your plan B. Accept that an imperfect result helps build the path to 'better', and 'better'. And you will also have the opportunity for learning, growth and vibrant glimpses of perfection every step of the way.

Critically, understand that you will — *will* — die with something still on your list to achieve. Everyone does. You can never nail down every opportunity, cross every t, dot every i. The list of 'to dos' expands exponentially according to how successful you are. Suck it up: you will never reach a point where you can say 'That's it. I'm finished. I won.'

So here are my proven tips to assist you on your less-than-perfect journey to get your art out into the world. And, I've not only had to coach others with these tips but I've also had to use them for myself!

1. GOSPA — Break the goal down into measurable, daily, achievable actions. If you're planning to run a marathon, then for today just buy the shoes or book a trainer or do twenty sit ups. But do something. If you're planning to write a book (and here we go with my ten years of perfectionism and the personal psychotherapy which didn't help much at first) then write a paragraph, write 300 words, write a chapter, write an article — but write *something* every day that takes a step in the right direction — and I mean, every day. Successful journeys are just an accumulation of lots of little movements in the right direction.
2. Remember Dr Carol Dweck's advice in *Mindset: The New Psychology of Success**, where she writes of the power of 'yet'. When the self-deprecating language kicks in and says 'I can't ... I'm not good at ... I tried, but it didn't work' just finish your sentence with 'yet', and exercise your willpower muscle.

3. Dweck also notes the importance of sharing your struggles, mistakes and key learning outcomes. An opportunity for learning is an opportunity to change to more of a growth mindset. So a great routine for the daily dinner is to share mistakes. 'What was your most interesting mistake today? What did you learn today?'

   While we're on the topic of family dinners, I also have to mention Shawn Achor's book, The Happiness Advantage' in which he mentions the Three Great Things. Just share, discuss and write down the three things that you're grateful for every day. It's brilliant!

4. Give yourself tasks where you *can't* achieve perfection. For example, many years ago I worked with a hugely talented risk consultant whose perfectionism was crippling his career progression. The 'no perfection assignment' that he set for himself transformed his life. Without (as he usually would) planning everything down to the last cup of tea, indeed, without even looking at a map or booking accommodation, he arranged two weeks' holiday, booked a mystery flight, packed his bags and his bike and went! This was the first of many 'no perfection assignments' and he was promoted just nine months later having largely cured himself of the need to be perfect. I was so impressed by his personal progress, that I actually measured it using a proprietary behavioural tool, to track his success over an eighteen month period. His behavioural profile actually changed radically and positively. I watched it. It was real. All he had to do was give up perfectionism.

   Now, if the idea of a 'no perfection assignment' sounds like too greater task then try Benjamin Mee's twenty seconds of insane courage.

'You know, sometimes all you need is twenty seconds
of insane courage. Just literally twenty seconds of just
embarrassing bravery. And I promise you, something great
will come of it.'
—**Benjamin Mee, Author, We Bought a Zoo**

5. If you haven't already, I encourage you to start writing a
   journal to assist you in re-training your brain.

   As prompts while journaling, ask yourself:
   - What's holding me back?
   - Where am I focusing my time?
   - What am I avoiding?
   - What should I be focusing on that will add greater value
     to my business or life?
   - What were my three great things for today?
   - What was my struggle?
   - How did I learn and grow today?
   - What risks did I take?
   - Did I try a 'no perfection' challenge?
   - Did I try twenty seconds of courage?

*Watch the turtle. He only moves forward by sticking his neck
out.*
—**Lou Gerstner, Chairman & CEO of IBM, 1993-2002**

Chasm closers

1. Choose positivity.
2. Manage yourself by managing your thinking. Remember, energy follows thought. So, challenge yourself: *How do I feel about where the business is, right now? How would I like to feel?*
3. Work on making better decisions. Use the ten-step decision-making process. Take the time you need.
4. Enhance your happiness. And your physical fitness.
5. Do away with perfectionism. Remember that Done is better than Perfect.
6. Use journaling to reinforce your brain re-training. Ask yourself: What were my Three Great Things today? What was my struggle? What was my most interesting mistake? What did I learn? What will I do differently next time?

And above all, never, ever, ever, ever, *ever* give up. It's a journey.

Stickability, remember?

Obstacle 6: Self Management

A bird's-eye view of the chasm

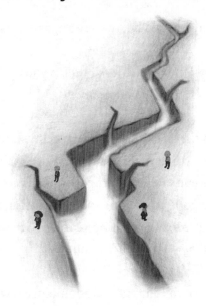

The big questions persist:

- What is life all about?
- Why are we here?
- What's this all for?
- How do I tell the difference between what is a successful life, and what isn't?
- And why try anyway?
- If I am successful, what does that really mean to me? And to the people I care about?

Well, here's a simple thought. Any job worth doing is worth doing well.

If you can see your life as a job — a work in progress — then it follows that 'success' isn't about being the best, it's about being *the best that you can be.*

To be the best that you can be, then clear goals are the first step.

And clear goals will not be achieved unless you apply the essential added discipline of *priority management.*

So on one side of the chasm we see the executive team and their extremely expensive external consultants with their strategy documents, their endless flip chart paper and their quarterly budgets. All with good intentions about delivering a significant increase in revenues for the coming year through increasing market share and new product development.

On the other side of the chasm are the employees who know the cold hard truth: that based on past results, even the best efforts of the serried rows of traditional consultants have failed to deliver to expectations.

The employees are brutally aware of the amount the business continues to spend on these 'god-like' external consultants despite the recent budget cuts and only a one per cent pay increase across the whole business for the coming financial year.

There are two significant challenges in this chasm.

Firstly, the consultants who are involved in the strategy development rarely continue through the execution phase. There's no accountability. And the concept of shared risk would be a show stopper!

Secondly, it's the executive team who own the strategy. And how do you maintain the level of accountability required within an executive team while also maintaining a healthy level of mutual respect within it?

How do the executives measure individual success and hold each other to account when the going gets really tough, especially without all falling out with each other? This is before we even tackle the cynicism of the workforce.

Deep in the chasm are the chasm-causers: the deep conflicts, the insecurities, the conversations that aren't happening. These are especially relevant with people who don't respond very well under the pressures of a tight market, a shaky economy, a missed deal or a mismanaged acquisition. Here is the profile of a business in crisis. As the boss, you absolutely need to take a bird's-eye view and determine your priorities, because if the chasm-causers white ant all the effort and activity going on, if you let them undermine you, then the walls can come crashing down.

The power of strive

'Doing' has its own magic contained within it.

The very process of striving towards our goals creates clarity, motivation and a real sense of fulfillment.

We start to feel more fulfilled, because as we progress towards the achievement of our goals, we begin to recognise our potential to achieve not only them, but also other goals and opportunities that open up to us as our horizons broaden. As we lift our eyes, the view improves and becomes more exciting.

So no matter how much progress we make, even just a little, there is always a sense of achievement, a sense of excitement, a surge of energy and an increase in confidence.

As our confidence increases, so does our energy and our ultimate happiness.

I have seen so many people achieve true happiness, peace of mind and outstanding results by clearly stating where they are going and how they are going to get there, and then by *starting*.

The ancient Roman poet Horace once remarked 'A task once begun is half finished.'

Nothing much has changed in 2000+ years.

So, you know what? It's not really about the goal (although that's always a starting point) but it *is* about the person who you become during the process of striving.

So: who would have thought that in a book specifically written for CEOs and their executive teams that I'd be talking about priorities and self management? You may even be thinking that this is a chapter to skip; that you have it all sorted out already.

Well, maybe you have. But I have noticed that the majority of my clients, no matter how senior, always have a bunch of 'impending priorities'. And these priorities are the real game changers for their organisations. In fact, as recently as today, as I write this, a CEO of a medium-sized business said that he wasn't yet ready to 'relinquish control' and delegate aspects of his role! He is so busy working on the detail of his business that his impending priorities permanently remain just that — impending. He just doesn't get started on them.

Priority management, self management, decision-making, will-power, focus, delegation, saying 'no': these are ALL areas in which we can ALL improve.

CASE STUDY

'Russell' is the Managing Director of a $115 million division of an insurance company. The first time I walked into his office I took photos of the mess: the piles of paper on his desk, the 1,962 messages in his inbox, the magazines and books on the floor and the message on his whiteboard (which he thought was funny) from his PA that said *Clean your office: find a home for all your papers. You DO NOT HAVE TO KEEP EVERYTHING!* **You can throw things out!**

Russell was keen to change his ways. He was up for a major promotion that would give him a greater global profile.

But it turned out that Russell didn't want that promotion enough. The second time I walked into Russell's office several months later, *nothing* had changed, except that he had moved his emails into a file where he wouldn't have to look at them. And as sure as night follows day, he is still marooned in the same position.

In my experience, if you won't do the little things, you certainly won't do the big things.

And this, by the way, is why it is so important to make sure that what it is that you are striving towards is predetermined, personal and meaningful. Otherwise, you will give up at the first hurdle.

So what does it mean to be effective?

Well, there is no doubt that we are all very busy. Being 'time poor' is so common nowadays it's a cliché. All those labour-saving devices we now employ have merely freed up more time to do more 'stuff'. We tend to work longer hours than ever before, and yet also do more with our leisure time than ever before. No wonder we sometimes get confused, or even exhausted!

So how effective are we at managing our energy and the twenty-four hours that we have in every day? Because there are never going to be twenty-five, no matter how much we wish it.

Many of us are in awe of those people who we perceive to be excellent at managing their time.

People who are always on time and seem to fit an incredible amount into their day.

They have a top job at work and a high profile, they study, they exercise, they have many and varied social activities, they are fully involved in family and community events, they give of their time to charitable and philanthropic activities, they always seem to be planning their next holiday, and they often run their own business (at least one, often more).

So how is it that these people always seem to have time for a cup of coffee and a catch-up chat? When meeting with them, they never complain or appear stressed about their lifestyle. In fact, they appear content, positive, satisfied, very happy and in control!

They drive us nuts! How do they do it?

Have you ever heard the phrase 'If you want something done, give it to a busy person'? Never was a truer word spoken.

People who manage their energy effectively take RESPONSE-ABILITY for their own success. They respond to opportunities by applying those abilities they have that are relevant. They give of their abilities freely. They take joy in applying them.

These are people for whom life is endlessly satisfying.

Now: think about the word 'satisfaction'.

The root of the word, Satis, is a Latin word meaning *enough*.

Add 'action' on the end of Satis, and you can see immediately that the ancient Romans were on to something.

'Enough' plus 'action' equals 'satisfaction'! (And don't pick me up on the missing 'f' in that equation; maybe it's just the expletive deleted that goes before action!)

Over the years, I have been fortunate enough to study the self-management habits of a variety of people from many different backgrounds.

There are characteristics that the most effective (and satisfied) people have in common.

The most obvious is a very clear vision that they talk about in the present tense and that they are passionate about. But there are a host of others.

Here is a long list of these characteristics. Tick the characteristics that align with your own. Don't worry if you can't tick them all — ninety-nine per cent of people can't — but highlight and prioritise the areas that you need to work on.

And then ask yourself which of these would you be prepared to implement immediately to generate immediate results.

The most effective and satisfied people in our society:

- have a clear personal vision and mission
- are action-oriented
- consciously maintain their health and energy levels
- think positively. Failing is not even close to their radar!
- set goals, make plans, and review their plans intentionally and regularly

- are always clear about what they are working towards
- document and review their goals on a regular basis with their family
- read and discuss their goals every day
- use visualisation and affirmation techniques on a daily basis
- realise that balance (peace of mind) is a priority for them
- give one hundred per cent to every area of their life
- allocate time to prioritised tasks and stick to the plan
- apply the 80/20 rule — they know which twenty per cent of their activity produces eighty per cent of the progress and they focus on that activity
- handle everything only once, adhering to the rule 'Do it, Delegate it or Dump it!'
- plan their day the night before in line with their goals and objectives so they hit the ground running
- spot when something isn't working, and fix it quickly. They're not afraid to look problems in the face
- are good at saying NO!
- are not afraid to ASK others for help
- behave ethically, with everyone

For 99.99% of people, success is not an accident. There is no such thing as coincidence!

Coincidences (and luck) are created by the things we *do* with our lives.

OK. So much for observable behaviour. What's the *thinking* that goes on inside you that makes 'good' behaviours possible?

Critically, what is it about your Thinking, Self-Talk and resulting

Behaviours that causes you to sometimes *ineffectively* manage your time, your day, and your life?

Maybe it is your thinking that has created an unhelpful habit. For example, if you find it hard to say NO to distractions from other people, is it because you are worried about not being liked?

If you get to the end of the day and often haven't tackled 'first things first', is it related to confidence in your own ability?

Do you 'not get through everything' because you are hiding in laziness and hoping against hope that your abilities will 'get you through'?

Are you relying on relaxation — drugs, alcohol, sport, socialising — to compensate for the frustration that comes from being badly organised, rather than tackling the root cause of the problem?

Is it because the distraction of minor crises (or major ones) — and thus being needed by others to solve them — give you a sense of self-worth? Nothing fires the ego like being needed.

Or is it that you are not a natural planner and 'things always work out for the best anyway'?

*Exactly what **is** it about your thinking, your self-talk and your resulting behaviour that needs to change for you to be more satisfied and effective?*

You cannot do this by being woolly-minded or cowardly in your self-assessment.

You need to examine your own self-limiting thinking and behaviours (and everyone has them) in order to derive strategies to overcome them.

This part of the process isn't easy. Thankfully, once you have got through this bit, it becomes easier, because good self management ALWAYS delivers positive results.

And results, on the path to the achievement of worthwhile, personal goals, always deliver added contentment and satisfaction and give us the energy to keep going! It's a self-fulfilling prophecy.

If you suspect that your thinking processes are somehow self-defeating, don't be frightened about going to see a professional psychotherapist to unpick how your thinking patterns have grown up (and then been translated into behaviours). This doesn't mean you're 'nuts', or that you are somehow a 'failure'. It merely means you are smart enough to recognise that there are experts you can consult whose one and only job is to help you better understand your own patterns of thinking.

Right, let's get down to the meat and potatoes

Think. If increasing your personal productivity could double the size of your business and dramatically increase your flexibility, wouldn't it be worthwhile changing your current habits? Do your own maths!

And if increasing your personal productivity could make your life more pleasurable, more fulfilled, better for your friends and family and you too, wouldn't it be worthwhile changing your habits? What really matters after all?

Efficient effectiveness

In my experience, the simplest trick to improving your efficiency and effectiveness is blocking your time and managing your activities in line with your goals and objectives.

Just like goal-setting, managing your thinking and use of time is a skill that can be mastered by anyone. All it takes is discipline and a little practice. By the way, get ready for some serious positive changes in your life. As you achieve more you will feel great, so it is not difficult to maintain effective disciplines once you actually get started.

OK, let's get started!

Remember the absolute basics!

- Release the Past. Get rid of Guilt, especially about past failure. Guilt is an immobiliser and a waste of energy. It solves nothing. Replace guilt with action. Choose to change and be more successful! (This applies whether you're twenty-five or sixty-five.) Everything that happens in our lives, good and bad, contributes to our understanding of who we are and where we're going.
- Be realistic about the behaviours and actions that you expect of yourself. You know what you need to achieve. So set your own standards, and don't adopt the standards of others.
- Communicate with clarity. If you choose to delegate, over-communicate!
- Wear hats. Rather than concentrating on trying to sort out 'work/life balance', simply consider wearing different hats during different times of the day. When you are with

your family, turn the bloody mobile and computer off and give your family your full attention. If you think you are so vital to the functioning of your business that you cannot take an hour to bath the kids with your mobile phone off then, with respect, you are sadly deluded. But when at work, stay focused. As Brian Tracy so aptly puts it, 'Work all the time you work.' Block your time, put on your hat and you will have created greater effectiveness without too much difficulty. The ideal *can* be achieved!

- Ask! Not asking for help is the biggest 'bloke thing' (rapidly and sadly being adopted by women who get through the glass ceiling) that gets in the way of success. Asking others for their support can make a momentous difference to your life — and theirs. Truly successful people — people who manage their time intelligently and deliberately — ALWAYS ask for help when they need it. They know that it is simply impossible to be Superman or Superwoman all the time. No-one knows everything, no-one can do everything. So … ask!

- If you are unfit or unwell anything else you do will be reduced in direct proportion to your level of unfitness or illness. Being fit and healthy is the most basic thing you need to work on. As a start, drink less alcohol, ingest less protein, walk more, sleep well, laugh a lot, and eat your veggies. I have known people's lives be transformed just by making these basic changes, and nothing else!

Quick tips to get you started on effective self management

It doesn't matter if you are twenty-five or sixty-five. The minute you improve these things, the more you will get out of life and you will be more contented and satisfied.

- Delegate whenever possible and treat your time like money. Look at your life: where *is* it that you need to invest your time to get the greatest return?
- Think of your desired annual income, then divide by 2,000. (That's the number of working hours in a year if you work an eight hour day, five days a week, and take a two week holiday.)
- Now take into account your hourly rate with *everything* that you do in your life (not just work). Is cleaning the house something that motivates you at the end of your working day? If not, consider other options. If your hourly rate is $400 and you can pay $40 an hour to have someone else clean your house, then do it!
- The same goes for gardening, car washing, supermarket shopping, groceries, handyman work, doing your tax return etc.
- Give *every* aspect of your life serious consideration.
- Work to your strengths and delegate the rest. This will allow you more time to concentrate on the business and on quality time with family and friends. The side benefit is reduced stress.
- Keep your goals close. Review them every day.
- Analyse your current time management practices. Track your time for one working week and then take some time to analyse it. Actually write down everything you did on a QUARTER HOUR basis. Now have a look. How did your use of time match your goals/objectives? (Warning: this can be quite shocking.)

- What prevents you from working to your high pay-off activities? What are you going to do about it? What needs to change? How are you going to change your current situation in order to manage and live to your own priorities?
- Start Now! Make a commitment to yourself at the end of every day and the commencement of the next, to living short-term activities according to your goals and objectives. Lots of 'little wins' add up.
- Plan more. Plan tomorrow at the end of every day. Plan the week ahead at the end of the week before. Plan the month ahead at the end of the month before. Plan your quarter ahead at the end of the quarter before.
- Prioritise your week, month and quarter activity lists in line with your goals and do first things first. Use the ABCDE method for prioritisation. (I'll explain that below.)
- Recognise and celebrate your successes! Review your activity list every day and look at what you have achieved. You may pleasantly surprise yourself!

Effective people start by finding out where their time actually goes. Then they attempt to manage their effectiveness and to cut back unproductive demands on their time.

This is a key understanding. Really effective people do not start with their tasks. They start with their vision and their available time. Then they fit their tasks into it. A raw 'to do' list can actually divert us from our goals. We need to check our 'to do' list against our vision and our available time rather than being ruled by anything and everything we can think of that needs doing. (Often, this means running around like a blue arse fly achieving *other* people's goals.)

Finally, they allocate as much time as they can, in a block, to each task. This is called 'time blocking'. They get into a flow on a particular item. Don't try and do five minutes on this and five minutes on that. Your brain won't keep up.

The next key to improving your personal productivity is to *focus* your energies on tasks that are urgent *and* important *first*. Understand that tasks can be either urgent or important, but are rarely, in my experience, both. When a task is urgent AND important it must be prioritised.

Most of us respond to the things that are urgent but not important such as comments from colleagues stopping by our desk, telephones, minor queries from the team, emails. All of these things keep us very busy but not necessarily productive and effective.

A few tips to keep you focused on the urgent and important tasks

- Prioritise your to-do list *the night before*. I know I keep saying it, but it really does work. Thirty seconds before you sit down at your desk is not the right time to decide what you are going to do with your day.
- Sleep on it. Then get to work early enough to *review* your list before getting into the day.
- Get stuck into doing the *urgent and important* things first.
- Block your time. Make sure you are doing urgent and important things and if you have a bunch of one type of tasks (for example administration) that are ALL urgent and important, do those together. Then all your urgent and important sales tasks, and so on. Bunching tasks by type

actually helps to maintain your energy levels because your brain is not constantly jumping from one type of task to another. But if a task is NOT urgent and important it doesn't make it into these blocks, it gets dealt with in the 'time for everything else' block.

- Don't say yes unless you ask when! When someone else delegates a task to you — and it is something you SHOULD be doing — then respond with 'My pleasure: When do you **really** need this by?' Encourage them to think professionally about the pressure they are placing on you and whether it is both reasonable and necessary.
- Close your door or go to a quiet place. Go out of the office altogether.
- Educate your peers and managers as to how you expect to be dealt with. For a start, set meeting times with strict agendas. If others are persistently late for meetings, then one day get up and leave, and return when they deign to call you and tell you that they have turned up!
- Communicate with polite clarity! It will save you a lot of time.
- Treat others the way that you would like to be treated yourself. Be courteous, helpful and prompt.

Develop a routine and discipline for emails:

- Don't use your inbox as your task list!
- Keep your email alert off. It distracts you and very rarely to good purpose.
- Limit checking your email to a certain number of times a day.
- Limit your inbox to one screen (maximum).

- File and manage incoming emails into folders.
- Use the subject line to provide as much information for the respondent as possible.
- State your objectives in the first paragraph of the email.
- Keep your emails succinct and use bullet points if they are helpful.
- If your email is longer than a screen, consider using a bullet point summary at the top of the email, or attach the bulk of the information in some other format such as an attached document or spreadsheet. People may defer or ignore emails that look too overwhelming.
- Wherever possible keep your emails SMART, especially when asking someone else to do something for you: Specific, Measureable, Attainable, Realistic and Time-bound.

The A-B-C-D-E Method

In his book *Eat That Frog*, Brian Tracy* says 'The more thought you invest in planning and setting priorities before you begin, the more important things you will do and the faster you will get them done once you get started.'

Brian Tracy's A-B-C-D-E method for prioritisation is a habit that I have formed to ensure that I achieve the things that are most important, every day.

The idea of eating a frog isn't very appealing is it? Often it's those difficult tasks that are actually the most important that we often put off, and we unintentionally sabotage our effectiveness. Now, if this is sounding like pretty basic stuff, you're wrong. I have worked with many CEOs and senior executives who put off the

A1 priorities rather than having to step to the very edge of their comfort zones. They are successful in other ways, but they duck this absolute necessity.

Visualising the yucky or difficult tasks as frogs to be eaten is useful. There are Executive Teams that I have been working with for over ten years who still talk about their 'frogs' and I have one passionate frog eater in the US who has put a value on his frogs!

Write your to-do list at the end of each working day. Then use the A-B-C-D-E Method to prioritise your list. This method helps you sort out the urgent and important from the urgent but not important, or the important but not urgent, so you plan a day that will generate the greatest results for you in a stress-free way.

A means 'Very Important and Urgent.' All A tasks must be completed today. These are the tasks that can make an immediate difference to your productivity and your results. The As are your frogs!

B stands for 'Important,' something you should do today if there is time. The B tasks are not as important as the A tasks but will become A tasks in time if they are not dealt with.

C stands for things that are 'Good To Do.' Complete these tasks if you have time BUT only once the As and Bs are completed.

Notice there isn't as letter for 'urgent but not important'. If something is merely urgent but not important you shouldn't probably be worrying about it at all.

D stands for 'delegate.' Effective delegation is not just about remembering to assign tasks to employees that fit within their current duties and responsibilities. To delegate is to give someone the *responsibility* for something that is usually part of *your* job and then to hold them accountable for their performance in delivering it.

I use the very simple SEED method for delegation which, if planned and delivered correctly, will work in your favour every time. (Don't worry, we'll get to the 'E' after 'SEED'.)

The SEED Method of Delegation

Scope

Once you have analysed the task and determined who would benefit from the opportunity to help you, scope out a plan to delegate the work. Be clear about the results that you desire by asking the following questions:

- What are the specific tasks that I'm delegating?
- Why am I delegating?
- What exactly do I want my staff member to do?
- Why did I choose them?
- What is their current skill set and experience?
- What training do I assume they will require?
- How will we measure success?
- How will we determine performance measures on the path to success?
- How will I measure my success in delegating?

Empower

Meet with your staff member and take them through your plan, determining clear, measurable expectations for the tasks being delegated.

Ask open questions to ensure that they understand what's expected. Questions such as:

- What do you perceive the potential challenges to be?
- How will these tasks impact your existing workload?
- What assistance do you envisage you will require from me?
- What sort of training do you think will assist you?
- How would you like me to communicate this to the rest of the team?

Depending on the nature of the task, training and regular reviews may be required as part of this process. Make sure that your expectations are documented *in writing*.

Entrust

You have delegated the task and given your staff member the opportunity to consult you at any stage. Now it's time to trust them. Make sure you've asked yourself, 'What's the worst that can happen?'

Design

Once your colleague is comfortable with the task, ensure that work plans and job descriptions are updated to include additional responsibilities.

I have heard every possible excuse for not delegating. Most often I have heard them from control freaks. From people who deal with their own anxiety by seeking to do everything themselves, to maintain a tight hold over information, to make plans unnecessarily obscure so that only they understand how important the plans are and how they are to be implemented.

I have also seen a lot of those people — inevitably — burn out. Or, very sadly, die young. Remember: delegation is about your health and sanity too.

OK, back to A-B-C-D-E.

E: Last but not least, E stands for 'Eliminate Whenever Possible.' These tasks will not have a positive impact at all on your productivity. Free up your time (and perhaps other peoples') by eliminating the E tasks altogether. Just dump them. If it turns out you were wrong to do so, it will become clear in due course, and in my experience it very rarely does.

Once you have prioritised using this method, you need to prioritise *within* these categories, of course. Your As and Bs especially need prioritising.

Don't be surprised if your day ends up being eaten up by As and Bs. That's OK. In fact, you could argue, that's the purpose of this exercise. Realising that some tasks are less vital than others and even never getting to them can reduce your stress, as you have a clearer idea of what *really* matters.

Now all this may *sound* very simple but the trick is to *discipline* yourself to use this method with your 'to do' list EVERY day and start your day with a healthy breakfast of frogs!

There's no way getting round one bit of hard work: your A priorities are always going to be the most challenging.

> *The things that matter most must never be at the mercy of the things that matter least.*
> —**Goethe**

CASE STUDY

When I first met 'Robyn', she was an executive search consultant specialising in technology. Robyn had her good months and her bad months which played out over a pretty average five years with the firm. By average, I mean that she was covering her costs but missing over half of her quarterly targets. Her CEO described Robyn as the cement in the team. She was fun to have around and was a mentor for some of the younger consultants. In effect, her continued existence had been justified and she was allowed to continue plodding.

The great thing for me in being an outsider is that I can ask the curly questions! 'What are your strengths? What's holding you back? What keeps you awake at night? What are the critical areas in which your performance could improve and make a difference to the business?'

Robyn's voice broke and a blotchy red rash covered her neck as she told me about herself. Robyn had never achieved the 'SmashIT' award (employee of the month) and had now lost all aspirations of doing so. She was nearly in tears.

In a workshop that same day, we discussed the 'frog-eating' concept and started drilling down on the A1 priorities for the following day, week, and month in line with quarterly goals and annual budgets.

The following month, Robyn smashed the SmashIT award and continued to do so for the following three months. The *only* thing she changed was focusing on her frogs!

It turned out that Robyn had a desperate need to be liked and found it hard to say 'no'. So she was easily distracted by the goals of others and had a terrible email-checking habit that eroded her productivity and, over time, her self worth. By focusing on her frogs, and developing a frog-eating dialogue in her team, Robyn put eating her frogs first and became a star.

Organising is what you do before you do something, so that when you do it, it is not all mixed up.
—**Winnie the Pooh**

Like many things, it is a matter of will

We are in a fast, fast world. The change during the last twenty years has been phenomenal. And the change affects our ability to concentrate.

Technology seems to be more interesting than conversations. Funnily enough, a taxi driver thanked me for taking the time to chat to him during a trip to the airport last week. In that moment I realised how lonely the life of a cab driver must be these days with the majority of passengers communicating to the world *outside* the cab or simply staring at some electronic device.

So, what is all this technology — the pace and variety of it — doing to our brains and our self control? This is something Roy F Buameister and John Teirney explore in their book *Willpower: Re-discovering Our Greatest Strength*.

For one thing, we are becoming overwhelmed by the intensity of brain activity that is now going on: the sheer multiplicity of everything we are expected to do and achieve. When all we had to do was milk the cows, then we put all our concentration and effort into that peaceful and rewarding task. But ask someone to milk the cows, *and* communicate simultaneously with three international offices, finish a couple of vital documents, tell their PA where to hold the Christmas party, keep abreast of international current affairs, and prepare for the parent-teacher meeting that evening, and we think the cow milking might become a less peaceful bucolic activity — and some of the cows would probably get mastitis.

According to Raumeister and Teirney, the first step in self control is to set *realistic* goals. Having realistic goals is not a weakness, it is a strength. Trying to achieve too much, in too short a timeframe, or to try and achieve the impossible, is self-defeating and depressing.

The second step is to create an environment to build your willpower and grow your self-control. Create the plans, enlist support, delegate if possible, look after yourself. It's all logical, and it's reiterative. The more you grow your self-control the more you will create the plans and carry them through successfully, giving you the encouragement and time to grow your self control, and so on, and so on.

While we're on this topic, here are some other wonderful pearls that I gained from Buameister and Teirney:

The *combination* of willpower and self-control are vitally important to success.

Willpower is like a muscle and it becomes weary as you use it. You use willpower for decision-making, problem solving, persistence, resistance. You can't be CONSTANTLY 'on'. It causes burnout.

If you'd like to increase your self-control, then exercise willpower regularly (and thus build your muscle) but do it in small ways throughout the day.

Be *conscious* of your willpower and when it's waning.

Develop the habits and routines that will regularly, gently dip into your willpower rather than the 'crash diet' metaphor of all or nothing. Some routine examples of things you can do that will help are a daily 'to do' list, blocking of time, regular check-in reviews, accountability meetings and journaling.

Don't create an environment where temptation will deplete your willpower. For example, turn off your electronic devices, turn off your email reminder, close your door, de-clutter your office.

Crash diets don't work. Band aid fixes don't work.

A progressive realisation of predetermined and worthwhile personal goals? Now, *that* works!

Chasm closing questions

1. Are you taking RESPONSE-ABILITY in your life?
2. What is it about your life that gives you the greatest sense of satisfaction? What areas of your life give you a sense of dissatisfaction?
3. What should you be doing more?
4. What should you be doing less?
5. Have you started? Are you 'doing'?
6. Are you fit and healthy?

7. Can you A,B,C,D, and E your tasks?
8. Do your tasks fit your vision and your available time?
9. What is currently distracting you from focusing on your most important tasks? What are you going to do about it?
10. What could you outsource or delegate allowing you to spend more time on your urgent and important tasks?
11. Name three things that you can do every day to improve your focus on the job. Write them down. Put them somewhere you will see them, to remind you.
12. What is the most valuable use of your time?
    a. Today?
    b. This week?
    c. This month?
    d. This year?
13. What do you need to do to get your life back into *balance*, starting immediately?
14. Are you content with your willpower levels? Are you aware of them? What routines could you implement to strengthen your willpower muscle?

Obstacle 7: Communication

A bird's-eye view of the chasm

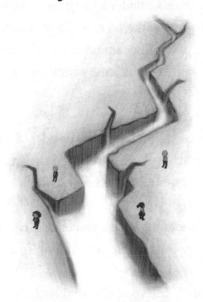

Leaders are often restrained by problems and decisions because of the risks involved in choosing a path to take. Sometimes many paths seem to have opportunities along them, or sometimes they seem to offer variations on a miserable theme. Often, choosing a lesser of two evils is part of the price of leadership.

Similarly, decisions are often made without enough time to think or consult: in the moment, under pressure. Such is life. And often this means without due consideration of the impact on the business, teams, communication and culture.

Leadership involves decisions. Leaders make decisions all the time. But how many of these decisions impact the organisation positively or negatively, in a measurable sense? Indeed, above the obvious headline level, does anyone actually bother to measure the results of decisions?

For the purposes of this chapter let's assume that a decision has been taken carefully. So now, on one side of the chasm you have the CEO who has taken advice from external consultants, the Board and his or her fellow executives, and his or her direct reports.

The decision and its impact has been considered and planned. A communication plan has been agreed and they have conveyed the decision and the reasoning behind it to all staff.

Yet on the other side of the chasm you have the employees who feel as though they have been overlooked and uninvolved.

Some choose to bitch and complain to their loved ones, others pour their guts out in quiet corners of the office, some are courageous enough to give their bosses some emotional in-the-moment feedback, while others just get on with the job with the 'We've been through all this before, and it's all about to happen again' attitude.

And each time it happens, they work a little less actively, and a little more resignedly, until, as surely as the tides on a seashore, they resign.

Regardless of how people choose to respond, it's these moments of *communication* that can make or break great organisations. If executive teams put as much thought into how they're going to communicate the outcome as they do into the planning itself, the whole organisation would be much better off, because how you communicate decides how people will feel.

> *I've learned that people will forget what you said, people will forget what you did, but people will never forget how you made them feel.*
> —**Maya Angelou**

Great leaders produce great cultures

A great culture creates the 'stickiness' that makes a business a great place to be.

Organisations are made up of individuals with different behaviours, learning styles and interests. And some people will always embrace learning more openly and enthusiastically than others.

So, to create stickiness within the culture of an organisation, you don't need people talking at people. You need a dialogue. You need to create a narrative that works for the largest possible percentage of individuals, more often, and more easily.

That dialogue can be delivered the way all the successful advertising campaigns are delivered. It's called multi-sensory learning and spaced repetition.

Your objective as a leadership team is to inspire and equip each and every member of staff by adhering to the following guidelines:

- CLEAR written and verbal organisational objectives
- CLEAR written and verbal individual objectives with 'no nonsense' articulation of the 'WIIFM' factor. ('What's In It For Me?' Remembering always that 'Me' is the person you're dealing with, not you!)
- CLEAR code of conduct. A vision and values document that is truly the way your business behaves, from the top down, not just a pious repetition of motherhood statements
- Two-way dialogue. Genuine discussions (possibly independently facilitated) that involve all staff and give them a voice
- Coaching (inside and outside of the organisational silos)
- CLEAR written commitments at the end of every meeting
- Structured workplace implementation with understanding and buy-in developed across teams and across management levels.
- Formal phased reviews in line with objectives.
- Support
- Reinforcement
- Performance measures for change (SMART goals and objectives)

When your business makes a change, does it adhere to ALL these simple guidelines?

OK. What does some of this jargon mean? Multi-sensory learning is simply the process by which an individual makes a decision on whether to engage with a project. It is both physical and intellectual, and engages all the key senses: auditory, visual and kinaesthetic.

Stages of multi-sensory learning

When people hear something genuinely new, they go through certain stages before they 'come onboard'.

Rejection: usually at the sub-conscious or habit pattern level.

Resistance: 'I'm ok here in my comfort zone'.

Partial Acceptance: 'Maybe there is something to this'.

Acceptance: 'Good idea but not really for me right now'.

Partial Assimilation: 'How can I actually use these ideas/strategies?'.

Active Assimilation: 'OK, I need to give this a try and see what happens'.

Understanding and accommodating this multi-sensory learning process is the starting point for creating effective communications.

To ensure that your key messages are understood and eventually embraced as their own, spaced repetition is vitally important. Spaced repetition is simply a posh phrase that means 'people need to be told things more than once to really get them.' (You might have spotted that some important things turn up in more than one chapter of this book. I'm not repeating myself for the sake of it. I'm using 'spaced repetition'.)

In advertising circles, for example, there is a rule of thumb that a radio ad needs to be heard three times before it sinks in.

Now that's not the whole story. As I write this it is the 50th anniversary of Martin Luther King's famous 'I have a dream' speech'. I don't think anyone who heard that even just once would ever fail to be inspired. But let's be frank: the changes we've decided to implement in logistics this month aren't quite as sexy, now are they?

So, for example, an inspirational MD that I work with shares the company values at every company event. In the early days, it was every Friday night at drinks. These days, with international offices, it's a little trickier, but he still manages to continue his regular values communication via the intranet, newsletters, brochures and video as part of the fabric of his occupying his role. He also tailors his message through sharing a story and presenting a values award that recognises the company's values in action. Most importantly, via the company's values and his values, his authenticity and passion shines through with every communication.

Another company has turned its 'secrecy culture' on its head and now broadcasts its Board meetings on the company intranet for all employees to watch, and to thereafter submit questions via email through their manager. They only turn off the cameras for reasons of deep confidentiality. How trusted and empowered do you think *their* employees feel?

Through multi-sensory learning and spaced repetition, every member of staff in a great business knows their company's values and the behaviour that brings those values to life. These businesses are nearly always 'fast growth' — of course!

It seems like common sense, yes? So why don't we all do it all the time? Answer: we are not *intentional* enough about it. We talk the talk on employee communications, but the pressure and complexity of our daily lives means we fail to walk the walk. If we truly believed it was as important to communicate the decision as well as make it, we would have much more productive organisations.

So, think about the impact that you want to have on your business that will ignite the engagement of your culture custodians *and* get you to your BHAG faster than you would have ever imagined. Is it worth planning for? Absolutely!

Some thoughts on learning styles

Each of us discovers and practises our skills in ways that are specific to our learning needs. This is anything but 'airy fairy' psychobabble. It is grounded in people's very real experience of working life.

People learn in different ways and no one learning style is necessarily better than another. In fact, most people combine different styles of learning according to the challenges they are being set. To make it even more complex, sometimes one learning style works well for an individual in one situation, but next time a different style will hold the key to them understanding what's going on.

So, how do you find your way through this maze? Simple. When it comes time to deliver a company-wide important message it is wise to use a number of different learning modes, including experiential, reading, writing, listening, observing, researching, drawing, story-telling and interviewing. That way you'll allow every member of staff to receive the key messages and themes through the combination of learning styles best suited to them.

This is particularly important in your messages relating to your policies and procedures, OH&S, values, vision, goals and objectives.

If you're not sure how to spread your message across different learning styles, and your internal communications team can't help, ask an external consultant. The small sum you invest will be more than repaid by better staff understanding.

CASE STUDY

One of the most memorable experiences in my career was working with an IT team in a business that had been acquired by one of their biggest competitors.

I arrived on site (after several weeks of preparation and interviews with the executive team) to find a group of thirty two recalcitrant, fixed mindset but highly intelligent employees.

Twenty employees were from the acquiring business, nine were from the acquired business and the extra three were contractors who told me that they were staying to work out their contract term and were on call so as to keep IT running throughout the conference!

The room was split accordingly and the atmosphere was as tense as a football dressing room at half time with the scores level.

My fellow facilitators and I agreed that multi-sensory learning, spaced repetition and appealing to the variety of learning styles was the only way to succeed in creating the stickiness required to start building *one team*.

By the end of Day 2, we had developed an ad campaign that the newly enlarged and integrated IT unit were to deliver throughout the business nationally.

They had their own logo, a buy-line, a brochure, and a video advertisement for all their internal communication.

Of course, it wasn't really about the advertising (although it certainly generated a lot of laughter and discussion throughout the whole business); it was clarity around the value that they bring to the business as a team. They now had a *shared* vision.

By forcing them to consider the communication of their vision to the rest of their business — forcing them to imagine they were talking face to face with every single employee to explain what they were doing and why — not only did they achieve greater clarity on what they had to do next to make the assimilation process really work, they also became enthused and co-operative.

The aim in creating a 'sticky culture' is to assist *every* member of the organisation in the transition from knowing (whether vaguely or explicitly) what they should be doing to actually taking a *series of actions* towards their pre-defined goals.

This always revives and invigorates teams, moving the maximum number of people from being process-oriented to achievement-oriented.

This process begins with you planning and delivering your key messages better.

Or in other words, setting an example.

Presenting your plans with impact

Many surveys suggest many people fear public speaking more than death! And public speaking when they are not prepared? 'Kill me now!'

This means, as comedian Jerry Seinfeld so appositely noted, that at a funeral most of us would rather be in the casket than giving the eulogy.

This fear stretches across all types of people and all levels of employment. I have seen otherwise charismatic and powerful leaders reduced to quivering jelly by having to take the mic when they least expected it.

Is the ability to grab an audience's attention and imagination only available to the 'born presenter'? Absolutely not!

In fact, of all the skills you need, effective public speaking that means you are not a quivering wreck when you walk offstage — whether that is externally obvious or not — and whether you are talking to your employees or anyone else is, ironically, one of the easiest things in the world to learn to be comfortable with.

Regardless of our occupation or seniority, few of us will be able to escape — try as we might! — ever having to give a presentation.

As the leader within your business, engaging and inspiring your staff may not be one of your written-down KPIs, but it should be. It's an A1 priority. And yet, so many senior executives are really average at it. I cringe when I see CEOs of massive corporations or organisations stumbling through, monotonously reading a boring speech that loses its audience somewhere around the middle of the first paragraph, or coming over on TV as stolid and uninteresting.

What a wasted opportunity!

Normally, it is sheer intellectual arrogance (or fear of admitting they need help) that prevents these people getting the necessary skill improvements to turn themselves into compelling and comfortable presenters.

As a result of a recent merger a few years ago, a new CEO was appointed. One of my clients, a talented and hard-working business unit GM, went to the new CEO's first 'presentation' to staff.

He sadly said that within fifteen minutes of seeing the overly wordy PowerPoint slides and listening to the CEO read his presentation notes from the podium (occasionally looking at the audience over his reading glasses) he knew that his future was not going to be with that business.

He said that he had a potent sickly feeling that his new boss was not someone that he would respect enough to stick around. He wasn't just uninspired, he was deflated.

Fifteen minutes!

Some research shows that an audience makes its decision on what you are saying in the first TEN SECONDS! How you walk to the platform. How you look up. How you stand. How you say 'Hello'.

So was his decision right? Actually, no. It turned out that his new CEO was a great leader but a crappy presenter. By then, though, the damage was done, and the GM had left.

How sad. How *avoidable*.

Every time you're engaging with staff, it's crucial to think about the impact of your verbal and non-verbal cues and the way you are influencing your audience — pinpoint any disconnect between what you *think* you're saying and what your staff are *really hearing*.

This is called *incongruency*.

When the verbal and nonverbal parts of your message are congruent, your audience hears and believes what you're saying. If congruency is lacking it's usually your words saying yes and your body language saying 'no'. The inevitable result is distrust and non-engagement. From this point on, rapport-building is extremely difficult to achieve. Just ask any failed politician.

Learning how to engage an audience goes beyond the standbys of simple control of nerves and voice projection — these skills are simply a means to an end. If you develop outstanding presentation skills you are able to present a memorable message that grabs the audience's attention through the impact of the delivery and the clarity of your vision.

On the face of it, there's not much to the task of presenting: just standing and speaking! So it should be easy, right? But we've all seen very good and very bad presentations.

Whilst it's easy to tell the difference, what *separates* the two may sometimes be harder to pick.

Presenting has fundamental principles.

Firstly, there is no one 'right way' to give a presentation. It will be as individual as you, your location (imagine the Gettysburg address delivered on TV and not on a battlefield), your objectives, and your audience. So a rigid formula would be useless, and many of us would categorise a formulaic presentation as a bad presentation.

When we're in an audience we want someone to genuinely speak to *us*, to communicate with *us*. As if they were talking to us individually.

We all have stories and experiences to share. An audience simply wants us to engage them with something that is interesting and relevant to them. In fact, research again shows that audiences are willing the speaker to do a good job. They are 'on your side' before you open your mouth!

Of course, much often rides on the outcome of a presentation. So if you seek a growing and impressive professional reputation and a sticky culture that makes hard work fun, you simply *must* be able to consistently deliver outstanding and effective presentations.

You just need the technique to make this happen. Try these tips:

1. Eye contact builds rapport and gives immediate feedback whether your audience is one or a thousand. So, don't get distracted by the dangerous 3Ps: Podiums, PowerPoint or Palm cards! They have to be used judiciously. Know your content and key messages well enough to connect with every member of your audience. If there's a power cut and you can't use PowerPoint, can you still communicate?

2. Speak conversationally, as if you were addressing each audience member personally.

3. How you stand really matters. Stand comfortably and with authority and remember to BREATHE regularly! If you think I'm stating the obvious here, I'm not. During moments of stress we often shallow breathe which further increases our stress levels. So, breathe from your diaphragm, deeply, and slowly. Take your time. Unless you have a really good reason to do otherwise, stand still.

4. Gestures can be distracting. Be mindful of where your hands are and use your gesturing to reinforce your messages. Make your gestures spontaneous. Avoid 'waving hand syndrome', or using the same hand movement to emphasise all the points in every sentence.

5. Make your voice dynamic. Vary your pace and pitch to suit the point being made. Think 'light and shade'. You can whisper to 2,000 people, you know!

6. Pause to emphasise a point. Then repeat it.

7. Typically speak louder than you normally would.

8. Slow down! The effective speaking rate in public is a maximum of eighty words a minute. Casual speech is more than double that. If you think you're speaking slowly enough, try counting the number of words you're delivering per minute, and then *slow down again*.

9. Prepare your presentation well in advance and know the start and end by heart, but don't memorise the whole speech. Simply be knowledgeable about the content and the key messages that you need to get across to your staff. You don't learn all conversations you hold in advance; you don't need to learn all your speeches line by line.

10. Include something personal. Everyone within your organisation wants to know more about you. Who you are, what motivates you, what you do when you're not at work. Share a little.

11. Keep it simple and err on the side of short, not long. Audiences will only remember ten per cent of your speech, and those will be headlines.

12. Include humor. Humor is entertaining and memorable. Humor makes you approachable. Humor can make a heavy topic easier to digest. You are not searching for belly laughs, but smiles and nods of recognition.

13. Smile! Smiling conveys confidence and enjoyment so it will simultaneously calm your nerves, and make you more likeable.

14. See yourself as the messenger. Focus less on you and more on your staff. Imagine how the information you are giving will benefit them. Believe in the message *and reinforce it with your story*.

Would you like to learn more? You can download a free e-book *Presenting with Impact* at www.iamtheproblem.com.au.

Now, I don't want to put too much pressure on you here but these 'presentation' moments are the key moments in which your staff and colleagues judge you, your success and the business's success. So, get some feedback. Is this an area that you really need to work on? Could you use a professional coach? (There are plenty around.)

The power of igniting belief

Charisma.

Oh, if only we could flick a switch and be charismatic every time we are in public.

What is charisma? Charisma is simply an 'aura' or magnetism that somehow attracts and interests others. Of course, the question is, where does it come from, how do you get it, and why does it really matter?

Charisma is about being comfortable — but not complacent — with yourself. You create charisma when your voice, body language and words create a big bundle of passion.

Charismatic people inspire others and act decisively without looking back.

The last part of the question — why does Charisma really matter? — is easier to answer than the others. It matters, because being a leader is one thing. Being a leader and having charisma is very much another!

You see, people with charisma always have a much easier job than those who don't. They seem to achieve more, with less stress and, often, in less time.

They are enthusiastically welcomed by colleagues, prospects and customers and described by others as 'someone they just enjoy being around!'

Most importantly, those with charisma very obviously enjoy their work more than those who don't.

So, it matters. Right then: where does it come from and how do you get it?

Charisma is generated by finding and filling a space. Plant your feet firmly on the ground, speak your truth clearly and patiently, and you'll create a fertile environment for opportunities to grow. You can do this regardless of your personality. Whether you're an introvert or an extrovert, you can consider what it is you want to communicate and deliver that.

Charisma comes from doing more than a mere 'needs analysis' based on research and active listening. To be charismatic, choose the moment and make a space for yourself in the conversation.

Listen to advice, but lead opinion. Provoke discussion. Seize responsibility; don't wait for it to be offered to you.

Charisma is about backing yourself. You won't always get it right, but always *try* to get it right. Learn not to take shortcuts. Give your all to the goal of getting it right.

Stick to what you believe in.

Of course, charisma is not without risk. Because of your belief in your own carefully considered point of view, you may seem to be intrusive. Others may call you arrogant. Nevertheless, the absence of charisma goes hand-in-hand with the absence of reasonable, considered risk-taking.

When dealing with a customer, for example, we know that from the very moment we embrace risk that we will either secure our place in our prospect's plans or we will walk out the door with no business.

Ask any boss what he or she wants most from his or her subordinates. They will nearly always say 'I want to know what they *really* think, not just hear what they think I want to hear.'

So if you're going to 'put your flag in the ground', timing counts.

Timing, as with most things in life, is everything. You'll need to have clear objectives for yourself, understand thoroughly what those around you are trying to achieve, and ensure you can back up your opinions with evidence.

One close colleague recently told me a story of the day he told the CEO of an important client that everyone in the business who worked for him was 'scared shitless' of him, and didn't dare tell him 'no' when they genuinely believed he was wrong.

The CEO was mortified. And my colleague knew that at that moment he risked being booted out of that business in short order. In fact, the CEO entered a short period of introspection, started working more closely with key colleagues, tried doubly hard to listen carefully to those around him, and along the way became much happier and more productive in himself. And my colleague? He was rapidly handed more of the client's business to look after. That's charisma in action.

Truly charismatic people use their honesty, their genuine empathy for their colleagues and customers, and their determination to make a positive difference to make others *want* to cooperate with them. The truly charismatic person in any field invites others into their glow of innate wellbeing — they are inclusive by nature. They want everyone to win.

Is charisma only naturally-occurring? Nope. I have seen non-charismatic leaders become charismatic over time.

This 'inclusive charisma' can be learned, developed, nurtured, practised, and refined.

However, it cannot exist in an environment when you don't really care about the people with whom you are interacting. Charisma, in the absence of genuine interest in others, is merely posturing. And people will see that. Within seconds, sometimes. It'll make them feel exploited and conned, not to mention disrespected. Falsely imitating charismatic behaviour without genuinely caring for those around you is one of the worst mistakes any leader ever makes.

If that all sounds a little scary, just have a go. Begin 'acting charismatic', develop a genuine interest in others, and observe the difference in the way that others relate to you. Choose to maximise your natural characteristics to your advantage.

One of Hollywood's greatest stars, John Wayne, was initially a bumbling, nondescript character stuck in minor roles in B grade movies.

Wayne began to analyse his every move and gesture. Nothing was left to chance as he re-made himself in the image he desired: riding boots exposed by ankle-length trousers, angled buttons on shirt-fronts exaggerating his otherwise narrow shoulders, the slow lop-sided walk and graceful movements, the infectious smile, the inner decisiveness in simply walking down the street. Above all, he allowed his natural good-nature to infuse his performances.

John Wayne was actually a nice guy and he simply let it show. He made every character he played a bigger, bolder, more closely defined version of the real him.

Eventually, his inner confidence expanded to fill out the created characters — because nothing was left to chance — and who ever knew? He became one of the most charismatic film actors of all time.

Do you have charisma?

Charisma is about perception, and a first impression often counts for everything, especially, as I have said, the first ten seconds of that first impression.

Little things really do matter — a clean car, good quality clothes, fit-looking body, (and if you can't manage that, a healthy one), a ready smile, clear eyes, firm handshake, friendly demeanour, pleasantly modulated voice. Above all, a genuine interest in those around you.

You'll be off to a good start if you surround yourself with charismatic people both professionally and socially. Watch them. Learn from them and you'll be encouraged to let your authentic self — and the things you're passionate about — inspire others.

Why bother?

Charismatic people build rapport very quickly from a first meeting. They generally have productive relationships. Doors are always open to people with charisma. They have more wins, they get more business, and get more done, and all more easily, too!

Charismatic leaders step out of their comfort zones and create positive images of how their products and services will enrich the lives of their clients and stakeholders.

Every time they step outside their comfort zone — successfully — then their comfort zone expands. So next time it's easier, then easier still, and then it just becomes second nature.

As they explain what they offer, they never make someone feel they are being sold 'to'. Instead they make the client or colleague feel like a partner as they convey their genuine belief in the benefits.

They encourage reciprocity by the manner of their interactions. 'We're in this together' is such an integral part of their belief set that they communicate it constantly.

In creating charisma in your life, remember, it's more important to create images in people's minds than words on a piece of paper. Charismatic people have a strong image in the mind of the people they work with.

No document, no presentation, no proposal can generate charisma. Only you — open, naked, vulnerable, authentic, empathetic and risk-taking — can generate true charisma.

What is in store for you if you don't develop charisma? Well, you'd better have the best product or the best price or the best service or the best team or the perfect offering, and even if you do, you'll still miss opportunities because some of your key staff members may simply prefer working for your more charismatic competitor!

You can do this. You can learn this. You can 'be' this. Because charisma is much more about who you really are than what you do or say.

Chasm closers

1. Create a dialogue. Be very clear and simple with every member of staff about your vision, BHAG, goals and objectives.
2. Use multi-sensory learning and spaced repetition to reinforce that direction in which you're heading, in line with your company vision.
3. Put as much effort into your internal communications as you do with your external.
4. Understand the learning styles of your colleagues.
5. Be very clear about the core messages that you want to deliver and the way that you want to be perceived in line with your goals and objectives.
6. Prepare. Think hard about your objectives every time you engage with others.
7. Give better presentations.
8. Do a check up from the neck up: get your head into the right space before you speak.

9. Be very clear, honest, direct and friendly. Be authentic.
10. Be aware of both your verbal and non-verbal communication.
11. Practise active listening. And think before you speak! (We often accept the logical answer to our question, but have we asked the right question in the first place?)
12. Think about your tone and the words that you use and your body posture and facial expression. Do they mesh with what you're saying? Are you creating congruence?
13. Slow down!
14. If you want to improve in this area, consider hiring a personal communications coach to provide you with some honest and constructive feedback and an action plan for improvement. A coach will help you to accurately identify the perceptions that you are currently creating and help you to develop perceptions that are consistent with the goals that you want to achieve.

Time spent on yourself is not a conceit. You're a better manager if you spend as much time and energy on yourself during your working life as you do on your holiday every year. (And by the way, you'll find that your holidays will get better and better, too!)

Obstacle 8: Behaviour

A bird's eye view of the chasm

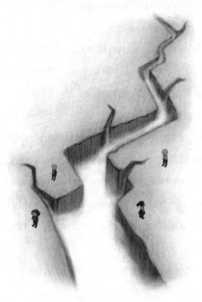

Behaviour is a universal language.

Watch the interactions between people, their gestures, their body language, their eye contact: how they 'deliver' their energy.

Forget minor cultural differences. In any country in the world, you can get a good idea of how a person is feeling just by watching them. What divides us is much less than what unites all human behaviour.

Wherever you are, you will also notice some similarities in how different people respond to each other. Some are friendly, chatty, interactive and effusive while others are more reserved, with little gesturing and eye contact.

By opening your behavioural eyes and being an observer of people, you are further investing in your ability to influence, persuade and lead.

Let's have a look at our typical chasm.

Nestling in the chasm today lie the timeframes, deliverables, expectations and a pressing deadline on the biggest deal this particular business has ever gone for.

On one side of the chasm you see the leadership team. Some have their doors closed, quietly going about their work as if there was nobody else in the business. Others are observably stressed, pacing the floor, leaning over the shoulders of others and discussing their work, agitated and short in their communication. One has gone off to play golf, and one has called in with a recurrence of the tummy bug that often seems to rear up right about now.

On the other side of the chasm are the employees. Some are obviously overwhelmed by the tasks in front of them. Some are over-talkative, some are sitting in silence with their headphones pressed firmly into their ears as they look intently at their computer screens. A couple are late back from lunch.

How you act now really matters — it makes a real difference to what happens next. If you want to stretch across the chasm and create a positive, focused team environment, it means being self aware enough to breathe slowly, suppress any tell-tale signs of agitation of your own, choose a neutral body stance, and to engage and ask open questions with sincerity and optimism. People need to know that you are leading. They make a judgement on whether or not you are by your behaviour.

Managing our inner life is one of our most difficult challenges. For one thing, it means constantly having an internal 'detector' on alert to gauge the emotions of others. And, even then, we can't always get it right.

For example, when first meeting one of my clients he described himself as upbeat and inspiring. But when I asked his Operations Manager for some feedback on his CEO's leadership style he said that he felt that his boss lacked authenticity. 'He says all the right things but never follows through.' Ouch: what a chasm, right there.

It's up to everyone in the leadership team to understand how your current leadership styles are driving the mood, the feelings, the culture and the effectiveness of the business.

That means it's up to you!

> *What is necessary to change a person is to*
> *change his awareness of himself.*
> **—Abraham Maslow**

One way to reach across: increase your magnetism

People are different.

Would you like to learn how to influence a wider range of people?

OK, start with this mindset. From the very moment that you wake up every day, your goal is to learn how to establish connections, accelerate rapport, and build trust with a greater range of people with various behavioural preferences. And to learn how to adapt your behaviour while remaining authentic.

Give yourself that goal, and wonderful things will follow.

Can you be sure? Yes, you can. Behavioural flexibility and increased levels of trust improves communication and overall performance. As was shown in Watson Wyatt's WorkUSA* research, companies with high internal trust outperform companies with low trust by nearly 300%.

Very often conflict can result from us misinterpreting the way people behave. Much of the time, this misunderstanding is because we interpret the behaviour of others, and therefore their motives, according to our own behaviour and preferences. Yet the people we are dealing with may be behaving towards us as they are for perfectly valid reasons that we don't even perceive!

For example, an extrovert may interpret introversion as being secretive, 'shifty', something to hide, anti-social and even downright un-friendly. Yet introverts may conversely view extroverts as shallow, bullying, dominant or aggressive.

In most cases the conflict is merely the result of an individual simply not understanding why somebody says something or does something in a particular way. Avoiding such misunderstanding is a key development in becoming a more successful person — a more successful *leader*.

If we are put off by different behavioural styles, we may unwittingly come to the conclusion that we will never resolve our conflicts with someone or within a team simply because we are different.

But this logic, which is a powerful and predominant life philosophy that many of us have unknowingly absorbed, is essentially based on the belief that different equals wrong.

In other words, if we have different opinions and views or different ways of doing things well, logically, one of us has to be wrong, right? This is simply because differences challenge and unsettle us.

This thinking is very common, even subconsciously, but is plain wrong. Never a truer word was spoken than 'it takes all sorts'. Through fear, we revert to the safety of the known and we reject, consciously or unconsciously, the behaviour of someone who processes communication and projects differently to ourselves. As a result, we miss the contribution of others who just have different behavioural or communications styles from our own. Worse, we may block them when they have the key to our future success.

The presumption that 'different equals wrong' means that our own judgments of others are often an unintentional cause of conflict. To move out of this type of thinking we need to see behavioural differences as simply that: differences. There is no universal law that says the way we do it, or the way they do it, is 'right'.

Different is just different. And when we truly respect another person, especially if we need their help, we will be willing to adapt our communication style to theirs in order to achieve maximised communication effectiveness.

There's a really good rule of thumb: the more flexible someone's communications skills become, the more influence they will have.

It's as simple — and as hard — as that!

Knowing me, knowing you

In your working life, you need to influence a huge range of people: customers, suppliers, colleagues, peers, superiors, subordinates and stakeholders. Your ability to influence others through the skill with which you manage your own behaviour will, in a large part, measure how effective and successful you are.

These skills are so important that vast research has been conducted in the area of inter-personal communication. Much of the research can be summarised into the following vital statements:

- We can't really make people do things — we can only influence their decisions.
- We buy from people we like.
- The way others treat you is a direct reflection of how you treat them.
- 'Nice guys' usually finish first — not last, as mythology would have us believe.

Learning a new language

The first step in building rapport and increasing your magnetism is understanding others and the way that they respond to their environments.

My introduction to the language of behaviour kicked off with a ka-boom in 1994.

I was running a division of a professional services firm. The administration support team, run by Emma, was the most productive, efficient administration team you could imagine or want. Whenever ideas were shared to increase efficiencies, Emma would be right onto it.

My relationship with Emma was alright but certainly nothing fantastic. I would often make the extra effort with Emma in attempt to build better rapport — I'd sit with her, go through reports together and try to get to know her better. But nothing seemed to work.

We organised a team workshop which included behavioural tools to help us better understand each other and our preferences.

Emma and I got the giggles when we started to learn more about each other's behavioural preferences — my preference being for a fast paced, people-oriented environment, Emma's preference being for a slower paced, task-oriented environment. I really enjoyed the fast pace of new ideas and lots of activity while Emma preferred to implement new ideas one step at a time making sure that every aspect was well covered.

Even though this memory is almost two decades ago, I can still remember looking at Emma's report and the words that spilled from my mouth, 'Oh Emma, I thought that you just didn't like me much!' She kindly reassured me that wasn't the case.

Thanks to Emma, this experience became one of my biggest tipping points as I went on to become accredited in a variety of behavioural tools and developed a new career as an Executive Coach.

We all have experiences like the one I've just described, and for some of us in the 'people' business, it's every day. We all know very quickly whether or not we click with someone or we don't.

In their book *Click*, Ori and Rom Brafman talk about that sensation that we experience when we meet someone for the first time and instantly connect.

As part of their research, Ori and Rom interviewed people asking them to describe the feeling in that moment. Many people described it as a magical quality. What's fascinating to me is that we often talk about these clicks as luck or serendipity and yet there are actions that we can take to create more of these moments in every interaction, if we choose to.

Sit in a coffee shop window for thirty minutes and do some people watching: the melodramatic driver and the not-so-concerned parking inspector writing up the parking ticket. The busy mum and the recalcitrant child. The bored business man and his overly enthusiastic colleague. No words necessary!

Interestingly, when we *don't* click and we have a feeling of awkwardness, have you noticed what happens?

For example (and excuse the clichés here as I crassly categorise behaviours to career choice) this interaction between the conservative, reserved pharmacist and the enthusiastic pharmaceutical sales girl.

Sales girl: 'Hi Greg. Great to see you again. I love the changes that you've made to the window display for the sun care range.'

Pharmacist continues with his task at the desk. No response.

Sales girl: 'I love what you've done with the display. It's going to be messy when it comes time to remove the sand from the window. Messy indeed. Looks great though.'

Pharmacist, not looking up, little gesturing: 'I'm filling a script Bethany. I will be five minutes.'

Sales girl: 'Great Greg. I can't wait to show you our new asthma range. We have an asthma pump which is the first of its kind.'

And on she cheerfully rabbited. OK, you get the picture.

As much as this is a real cliché, it was real. I know it was real because I was the customer getting the prescription filled! Little did Greg and Bethany know that I was loving every minute of their little show which has gone on to become an illustration for many of my behavioural workshops.

What happens when we don't click (and as you know, this happens more often than not), is that we become more rigid in our behaviour. In the case of Greg and Bethany, Greg became more reserved with no eye contact, little gesturing, staying on task. Bethany became more excited hoping that her energy might rub off on her prospective customer. Greg's continued reservation just increased Bethany's enthusiastic, chatty style.

What about you in your role as leader? Do you expect your subordinates to adapt because you're the boss? Ask yourself: whose responsibility is it to lean into the cracks with chasm potential? Are you going to remain true to your style or try some behavioural flexibility on for size?

Like bees to a honey pot

And then of course there are the magnets.

These people are quick to build rapport because they are high self-monitors.

They have a high emotional intelligence. They are more aware of the attitude, behaviour, emotions and mindset of others and are able to adapt accordingly. And by the way, because they have extra 'clickiness', they feel more comfortable and fulfilled in themselves, too.

The great news is that you can *learn* how to increase your ability to adapt:

1. Open your behavioural eyes. From the moment that you meet someone for the first time, observe their behaviour. Are they fast-paced or slow? Are they loud or soft? Do they use short sentences or long? Are they reserved or effusive?
2. Lean into their world. If they're softly spoken and reserved, slow down your pace, take your time, concentrate on your

breathing. Listen hard — they are weighing what they say. Show you respect them by doing the same. Suppress any impatience. If they're friendly, casual and relaxed, take some time to be social instead of getting straight down to business. If they immediately start talking business and you're usually more social, try holding back a little; be open, engaged and willing to connect on a level that the other person prefers.

3. Authenticity. I'm definitely not suggesting that you should try and become someone that you're not. Rather, I'm suggesting that you become more aware of the other person's needs throughout the process of building rapport, and adapt to those. Concentrate on your breathing — almost always, make it slower! — and take note of their pace and style. Over time, this will become more natural and you will be quicker to develop rapport with a range of people with whom you wouldn't have otherwise have 'clicked' quite so well.

4. Remember that people with different styles often make the best teams because they complement one another's skills. It's worth thinking to yourself, 'I have to work a bit harder to click with 'A' but he always delivers me more insight and better work than 'B'. It's worth my while adapting to him.'

The most important determinant of the sale

IBM conducted a survey many years ago in which a wide range of companies across a variety of industries were surveyed to determine what was the single most important factor in a sale, or, indeed, any business transaction.

They found it wasn't price, it wasn't the quality of the product or service, it wasn't the reputation of the organisation, nor was it the skill, competence or even expertise of the salesperson or service provider.

What they found was that in over eighty per cent of cases the single most important determinant of the sale was the relationship developed between the two parties.

There are a number of ways we could respond to this statistic.

On the one hand, and very commonly, we could feel confused or shocked. I often hear things like:

'My clients tell me what they love about our product is its quality. We have spent a lot of money developing the best product on the market. That's our competitive advantage.'

Or: 'We provide a service equal to or better than our competition and yet we are significantly cheaper. This has driven our market share.'

These competitive advantages are fantastic, no question. But why do we look for such mundane explanations to explain success? It's quite simple. We look to these factors because they are tangible, quantifiable and measurable. But they don't reveal the actual experience of buying, which incorporates other factors that are intangible, subjective and much more difficult to measure.

But if the statistic is correct — it has been repeated in many other studies — and if you can *really* understand its impact on your organisation and the way you interact with your staff, clients and other stakeholders, then it can become extremely empowering because the good news is you can always improve your relationships.

No relationship is perfect. They can all be improved.

And you can do this immediately. It doesn't require anything more than developing a better understanding of what your staff, your leadership team, your customers, your suppliers and other key stakeholders *really* want — both their explicit and implicit needs.

How? By being more aware of your behaviour with other people. You can build better rapport and find out more. We all can.

Increased rapport will lead to increased trust, openness, greater effectiveness, better decision making, longer term satisfaction and loyalty from your staff. In other words, a sticky culture.

For example: some people are just instinctively more anxious than others. It might be their life experiences. It might be their brain chemistry. It might be fears that are pressing on them.

When you are dealing with that person, whether they're a co-worker or a client or whomever, it is a perfectly legitimate use of time to regularly establish and re-establish calm and reassurance. The product *will* do what it's supposed to. The service *will* come up to scratch. The plan *will* have a successful outcome. The re-organisation *will* achieve its goals. He or she *will* be alright.

'We're in this together. You have my commitment to it working. You're not alone in this.'

A leader takes other's anxieties on themselves, and offers solutions. A leader doesn't brush them aside with irritation.

You're a smart cookie. You know that people are different and have different needs. You can understand their needs by identifying their behaviour and thus what motivates them to higher achievement, or what reduces their motivation.

Spend some time doing an audit of yourself. What are your preferences? Do you have a preference for people or tasks? Really *think* about it, because we all have preferences. Are you fast paced in decision-making and responding to your environment or do you prefer to think things through carefully? Do you sometimes switch between behaviour modes — people do — and thus run the risk of confusing people? Why do you change behavioural modes? What are the stimuli that lead you to behave one way or the other?

What about your stakeholders? What are *their* preferences?

If you can increase your self-monitoring and learn to adapt your behaviour to different audiences you will naturally, over time, increase your ability to build rapport, influence and lead. You will become more magnetic.

The driving WHY!

Many studies have shown that we actually retain a maximum of twenty-five per cent of what we hear for forty-eight hours after we hear it! (And in fact it may be less than this. Certainly in any speech-making situation you'll be lucky if your audience retains any more than ten per cent.)

242

So the most successful presenters create a need and arouse an emotion in the audience through active involvement and participation from their very first point of contact to ensure that all their major points are remembered, and above all, that they leave the right overriding impression upon their listeners.

As mentioned in the chapter on Communication, during any conversation, (and a presentation is just a specialised form of conversation), people will make choices based not only on the hard facts they hear, but also on emotion, inspiration and vision.

Therefore, while it is important that you know what you're talking about, it is just as important that you truly know your audience — staff, customers, stakeholders, the public — and you can show that you really care about them.

So as a start, be really clear about your WHY!

Placing your WHY front and centre in your communication behaviour is a great way to create empathy, because it means you are dealing authentically with people. They get what you are about, so they can sort you into the right compartment in their mind for dealing with you.

Your WHY is your driving purpose for coming to work every day. It's your big picture reason, it's your motivation, it's your driving force. It's where your mojo resides. Your WHY is the reason your future employees will be joining your business. As Simon Sinek said in his book *Start With Why*, people don't buy what you do, they buy WHY you do it. So share your WHY!

During a recent values workshop, I asked the CEO of a health organisation to share his WHY with the staff. He came straight out with 'To increase the life expectancy of people living in the bush.'

He went on to share his story and choked up (just a little) as he talked about health outcomes for people living in remote communities, and as I looked around the room I noticed that every person was engaged in his WHY as though it was their own. I saw real emotion in their eyes.

My WHY, for example, is to make a real, tangible difference to business culture so that when small businesses become big businesses — or when big organisations of any kind need to change direction — they do it with integrity and compassion for every member of staff, making 'work' a truly connected, networked community, not just 'jobs for a wage'.

Not only is this great for productivity and profits, it's the type of world I want to live in, and that I want my children to work in. I want to leave the world a better place than I found it, organisation by organisation.

My WHY drives me every day because I believe that the soulless corporations in which some people are forced to live, day in, day out, erode people's self worth and create a sadness that permeates families, communities and societies. They are like a cancer, destroying productivity, getting in the way of meaningful change, and causing misery.

Creating a genuinely connected place to work is a much more appealing option!

So, what's *your* WHY? Do you know it? Do you communicate it, with enthusiasm and passion? Do you adapt your communications style and behaviours to ensure that other people share it? Or do you keep it to yourself?

Let it out! Free your WHY!

Understanding Motivation

To further explore behaviour, it's important to understand the motivation and thinking behind the behaviour you're observing.

Professor Tory Higgins, a psychology professor at Columbia University has conducted a body of research on what's called Regulatory Focus Theory (RFT)[*] which is a study of people's perceptions and responses in the decision-making process in the pursuit of their goals. Here are some tips that you as a leader will find very interesting: as I explain in the culture chapter, the goals that bring out peak performance are the goals that satisfy at least one of our basic needs. Those being:

- Belonging
- Competence
- Autonomy (while doing things that reflect our values and beliefs)

If your behaviour is aimed at achieving a goal that satisfies all three needs at once, there will be no stopping you. For example, one of my clients participated in a marathon last year. I almost fell over when he first mentioned it because he was extremely overweight and a smoker. Not exactly marathon material, or so I thought.

As it turned out, the marathon satisfied all three of his basic needs. He had the opportunity to train four times a week with his colleagues (belonging), he was improving his health and wellbeing (competence) and he was matching dollar for dollar with the monies raised for a worthy cause (autonomy).

If your people are satisfying all three needs, they will be supporting you brilliantly!

It's interesting that the majority of us pursue popularity, fame, wealth, 'stuff' to make us happy, but these things only sustain us short-term. For meaningful, worthwhile, sustainable happiness, pursue the goals that satisfy at least one of the three basic needs, and preferably all three.

Playing to win versus playing not to lose

Higgins' research validates that when people play to win, it's about risk taking, creativity and innovation. This is called Promotion Focus. When people play *not to lose,* the mind set and decision-making process is different — it's about accuracy, compliance, risk mitigation, being a careful planner, not making mistakes. This is called Prevention Focus.

Shifting mindsets

For your business to be highly successful, you need innovation, creativity and idea generation. But Promotion and Prevention both play a valuable role in our behaviour.

For the phase of ideas generation, the Promotion focus mindset works best because the thinking is essentially positive. It's about the possibilities. At the evaluation phase, Prevention focus works best because you're getting down to the practical application of your idea and using sensible caution.

It won't surprise you to know that some people get stuck in either Promotion or Prevention. Bad idea. If you find it hard to switch from one mindset to the other, the answer is blindingly simple. Appoint a senior empowered colleague whose role is to balance you. Oh, and listen to them, too.

Look around your current set up and start observing the behaviours of you, your Board and your executive team. Are they more prevention focused or promotion focused? Are you too biased one way or the other? Are you adaptive, or stuck in one trait?

Consider adapting your communication behaviour in order to better get your key messages across to certain audiences. For example if your chairman is Prevention Focused but you need to increase your budget by twenty per cent, how would you adapt your concentration on Promotion to convince him of your plans? How can you adapt your behavioural style to reassure him?

Remember: people do things for *their* reasons, not yours!

Chasm closers

1. Describe the characteristics of the people you enjoy dealing with the most.
2. Describe the characteristics of the people you least enjoy dealing with.
3. How do you need to adapt your behaviour to develop better productive relationships with all these people? What action are you going to take? Remember, we tend to gravitate to dealing with people we like the most. This can be a trap if someone else we find a bit more difficult actually has the magic key we need.
4. And also remember, if you really like dealing with Person A then you might *need* someone with a different style — Interloper B — to disrupt your cosy rapport with A, in case you and good ol' A are just enjoying reassuring each other a bit too much!
5. Practise deliberately adapting your behaviour, and building rapport, with people who you find challenging. Usually

these are people who have a behavioural style that is very different to your own.

Go to my website and download the Self Awareness Check.

6. Clarify and communicate your WHY.

There is a fair amount of underlying rigidity in our personalities! Even recognising this rigidity is further along than most people get. Getting rid of it is a huge step forward.

So: are you genuinely interested in finding out more about your behavioural style and improving your ability to build rapport? You want to be 'a magnet'?

Encourage your colleagues and direct reports to comment on your communication behaviours and urge them to be bluntly honest about any areas they find tricky.

Create safety for them to be completely honest. They may tell you something that changes your world for the better.

And perhaps work with an executive coach using a behavioural tool. Align your key development areas to your WHY and you will be immediately more mindful, as I freely confess I have been since my first experience in this area twenty years ago. And more successful. Oh yes, and happier, too!

Obstacle 9: Curly Conversations

The bird's-eye view of the chasm

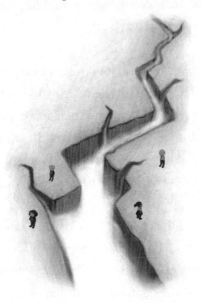

Think back to the last time that you left something to fester.

A conversation that was left or swept under the carpet, hoping that things would improve over time or dissipate. What was the outcome?

Usually, things just continued to fester, right?

Let's look at our chasm again. On one side of the chasm you have your fellow executives who get on with the job, working hard to get things done, reacting to day-to-day operations, inspiring the staff and growing the businesses in the only way they know how.

In the evening, when they have a few moments to reflect, they ponder on the day, complain to themselves and sometimes their loved ones about what went wrong, and how things could be better, if only people would listen.

And, most of the time, in my experience, their biggest challenges come down to the curly conversations that have been left unspoken at the office.

Often these conversations relate to the overwhelming, ongoing challenges that they have with their easily distracted colleagues, their golf-playing fellow executives, their incompetent CEO, their interfering, meddling Board, their distant disinterested Board, their incompetent direct reports, their belligerent suppliers, their show-stopping, initiative-destroying CF'NO'. And so on.

On the other side of the chasm is an organisation of workers wanting their place of work to be a happier place, knowing full well that there are some issues within the upper ranks of the business that they don't quite understand. They see a dysfunctional leadership team, but don't discuss it very often. They find it difficult to understand and feel powerless to do anything about it.

Instead, they just get on with their jobs, head down, bum up hoping that, in time, things will be better. And if it isn't, well, they'll just stumble along, unproductively, or they'll leave, taking their accumulated knowledge and confidential information with them.

Across the chasm, a lot is left unsaid. People make their own minds up as to what's going on. The employees hear the raised voices, notice a door being closed just a bit too fiercely, see the eye-rolling, the shortness of breath and the flushed faces when members of the executive haven't delivered on a promise, when they are late (yet again) to a meeting into which they sweep with bundles of self-importance, when they have a long business lunch they shouldn't have and defer a performance review or a problem-solving session that the employee has been hanging out for.

As always, the executives on one side of the chasm and the workers on the other all have the same goals for the business. They would all love work to be something that they really look forward to every day.

And the most ironic thing? The chasm closer is often only a frank conversation or two away. But, time has gone by — months, maybe years — and the idea of actually having the curly conversation suddenly seems insurmountable.

A great model for successfully carrying out 'Curly Conversations'

For twenty years I've found the GROW model to be extremely helpful in preparing and implementing a structure for curly conversations.

In my experience, a looming, otherwise 'curly' conversation is all about planning, planning, planning.

GROW simply stands for Goal, Reality, Options and What Next?

A GROW plan helps you to ask the questions to help the person with whom you are having the conversation to find the answers within themselves. It helps your colleague to see the big picture, the impact of the situation and their role in the outcome. By developing the habit of GROW you will be much clearer in your thinking and communication and successes will come more easily.

The GROW model was developed by Graham Alexander, a business coach, along with Sir John Whitmore, a motor racing champion. It is described in detail in John Whitmore's book *Coaching for Performance, The New Edition of the Practical Guide**.

GROW was used extensively during the 1980s in the UK for coaching conversations. In doing a web search on the GROW model today, I was presented with 76,700 results. So, GROW has become very popular since it's inception. It has stood the test of time.

So, how does it work?

You can plan and deliver your curly conversation using the GROW table on the following pages. You also need to consider the following points:

- Be as specific and succinct as possible.
- Keep the emotions and your opinion out of it. State the facts as you see them. Be clear about what it is that you and your colleague are both working towards.
- Breathe! It's not uncommon for our breathing to become short and shallow on the verge of a curly conversation. Be conscious and slow it down. As you're walking into your meeting, take a deep breath and exhale slowly.

- Be mindful of your body language. Keep your back straight and maintain eye contact throughout the conversation. Think of your energy flowing up and out from your diaphragm.
- Keep your main GROW points close by if you need to. We can all do with an aide memoire, especially in stressful situations.
- Slow your pace down — way down — and remember to use open questions and listen. Be prepared in advance to be comfortable in the silence once you ask a question.
- When you find yourself caught up in the detail or losing direction, go back to the goal.

Often, these are the conversations that can take us off centre. What is it that you need to do to re-centre yourself? Pause. Posture. Breathe. Listen.

The GROW table on the following two pages will assist you in planning and delivering your conversation. The questions have been refined over many years and they are guaranteed to take a conversation from curly to straight and compassionate within minutes. I have clients in senior executive roles all over the world who have gone as far as laminating these questions. And, I know of a few people in the emergency services sector who use their laminated GROW questions to confidently deal with the unexpected high-profile situations that they find themselves in at a moment's notice.

GROW is brilliant. Use it.

Personal Planning

GOAL

Purpose & structure of conversation

What's the goal?

What do I want to achieve?

What would be a measure of success for both of us?

What will be different as a result?

What am I working towards?

Why is this important?

REALITY

Share your observation — facts, feedback & impact. Seek *their* perspective

What's the situation right now? (facts, data)

When did this begin? (dates, times)

What additional information do I need?

What else is relevant?

What have I tried before?

How do I need to prepare?

What are the obstacles?

Who might help me to prepare?

OPTIONS

Possible solutions. Generate ideas for change & growth

What are my options for achieving the goal?

What are the obstacles?

How might I approach this situation?

What other options do I have?

Knowing what we know, what else might I consider?

Which option will get the fastest results?

What is the risk (of this option)?

WHAT NEXT?

Next step, timeframes, resources, follow-up, commitment

What are the immediate next steps?

What actions need to be taken?

How will I know it has worked?

Who will I get to help?

How would I like them to help me? When?

Do I have a plan B?

Conversation starters

GOAL

Purpose & structure of conversation

What I would like to achieve today is ... How does that sound?

The reason for today's meeting is ... What would you like to achieve today?

How will things be different as a result of this meeting?

How can I help you today?

REALITY

Share your observation — facts, feedback & impact. Seek *their* perspective

I'd like to outline my understanding of the situation. Is that okay with you?

What *is* the situation? How do you see it?

Who else is affected? What might their perspective be?

How are you feeling about this?

What else do you / we need to consider?

Can I outline my understanding of what you've said so far so that I'm really clear?

OPTIONS

Possible solutions. Generate ideas for change & growth

What options have you thought about to address this situation? How about we brainstorm these and other options together?

I have a few additional ideas to share with you. Is that okay with you?

How else might you/we take this forward?

What are the potential obstacles or risks?

Knowing what you know, which option do you feel would be the best approach?

WHAT NEXT?

Next step, timeframes, resources, follow-up, commitment

What Immediate action needs to be taken?

What's the timeframe?

By who?

By when?

Agreed follow up date?

Here's an example:

Situation

Clive is the head of marketing and communications. He has been a member of the leadership team for almost 7 years. In recent months he has been arriving late and appears generally disengaged. Additionally, Clive's emotions have been running pretty close to the surface and he has lost his patience on more than a few occasions. There has been one formal complaint and two of Clive's direct reports have resigned this week. He didn't turn up to last night's executive team meeting and, not surprisingly 'Clive' became the first topic on the agenda! Julie, the CEO has been given the task of 'fixing' the situation quick smart. Julie is nervous because even though she's the CEO, Clive is a majority shareholder who she wants to keep on side. Curly enough?

Goal

I'd like to help Clive to understand the impact that his behaviour is having on our culture. I'd like to walk away with a plan to assist Clive, and all of us.

Reality

The situation is that there has been a significant change in Clive's behaviour.

Since early February there have been several incidents both in the office and on client sites that have impacted staff morale and customer service. There has been one formal complaint and two resignations from Clive's team. I have met with Clive regarding each incident and there has been little improvement in his behaviour.

I really want and need to understand what's going on for Clive. In the past, when we have had these conversations, Clive has taken full responsibility and apologised. In preparing for this meeting I am going to focus on asking open questions and getting Clive more involved in the Reality and Options of GROW.

Options

Last time we had one of these conversations, I was specific about each incident and the impact. Today I'm going to suggest getting HR involved, and maybe providing an executive coach or a counsellor. I will also ask Clive to suggest some options too, so he 'owns' the solution.

What next?

Clive and I will discuss the support that he requires. I will also ask whether others need to be involved and arrange another meeting for tomorrow to agree on a development plan.

The Meeting Itself

Here's an example of how Julie's meeting with Clive may unfold to assist Julie in addressing her goal. As you will see, it's all about taking the time to plan several open questions to get Clive talking:

Goal

Clive, during our meeting today, I'd like to better understand why there has been a shift in your behaviour and what we can do to assist you in better managing your responses to conflict and stress in the workplace. What would *you* like to get out of our conversation today?

Reality

Clive, this isn't the first time that we have had this conversation. You've been arriving at the office late. We often don't know where you are or how to contact you. You didn't join us at last night's meeting and we have had a formal complaint through HR.

Clive, what has been happening?

Has anything else been going on that could be relevant here?

Options

Clive, you're important to this business. Help me to understand what we can do to address this situation.

What have you tried since our last conversation?

What will happen if we don't address these issues and your behaviour continues?

What options can you suggest that will positively impact your behaviour?

What have I not asked you that *you* think I should have asked?

What Next?

Clive, I want to thank you for engaging with this process. Let's be honest, it's a bit stressful for both of us.

I'd like you to consider the options that we have discussed today. How about we meet again in the morning to discuss a development plan? How does that sound?

Did you notice that after plenty of good, encouraging open-ended questioning, Julie actually wrapped up with a closed question? Clive's only option was to say 'Yes' or 'No' which facilitated the opportunity for Julie to achieve her goal for the meeting.

Whenever conversations get really curly, try and stay calm and go back to your goal. You know those moments when things are not feeling quite right. You may feel your heart rate increasing or an element of discomfort in your eye contact or their body language.

It's easy to let these moments pass in the hope that it's just a one-off. I'm here to tell you that every moment is a crack. It's not of huge significance right now but left undealt with it *will* be — one day in the future, and possibly not too far away, either.

Ironically, you and your colleague have the same goal. Human beings are innately co-operative beings. We want to get on, and we want to work to mutual goals. You both want the business to be successful, you both want your staff to enjoy coming to work every day. You both want to be significant contributors to the overall success of your teams, your clients, your service providers and your future.

And yet, it's the little things that undermine our success. The things that we should have, could have, would have said in the myriad of moments — but didn't.

Instead: choose to GROW.

Happy parents make happy kids

Like happy parents make happy kids, so too do happy Directors make happy cultures.

Let's face it, going into business partnership, joining a Board or a senior executive team — these are all not really that different to getting married. In fact, we often spend more time with our business partners and fellow leaders than we do with our life partners.

OK, this may be the most obvious statement in this book. And yet, we let the little communication cracks emerge with the people who are the most important in the grand game of ensuring that the business is a huge success!

It's comfortable, it's easy, it's habitual and preferable to address the easy stuff and leave the harder stuff for another day. Or maybe never.

But as a leader in your business, you are a culture custodian, an advocate and ambassador. Letting the communication cracks emerge, not having the curly conversations is impacting your culture, your revenues, your relationships inside and outside, and it's reducing your profits. Guaranteed.

So, what's holding you back? If you fear to have the conversations that may cause you discomfort and criticism, you will never create the culture that will bring you the success that you're after.

C A S E   S T U D Y

Craig, Damian and Susan have been co-directors of a professional services firm for fifteen years. What brought them together in the first place was their niche skills in financial services and shared values. Until three years ago, they had all been living a bit of a dream, loving what they do every day, working alongside like-minded people and making more money than they could have ever thought possible.

Damian is in his mid sixties. The patriarch of the group, he still loves the work, he still puts in the hours but is less involved in the daily operations of the business.

Everyone knows Damian's daily grumble (which was funny once) that he is at the point in his life where clients and staff get in the way of him getting his work done. He often smirks as he utters the often-repeated words: 'If it wasn't for those bloody clients, our day would be so much easier.' Needless to say, when Damian is having a good day, things are pretty quiet around the office. When Damian is having a bad day, the whole world knows about it and there's lot of angst within the executive team.

When I first met the executive team, my directive from the CEO was to get Damian 'back on the bus' and get him excited about the future — the way things used to be.

But of course the world through Damian's eyes was very different!

On one side of the emerging chasm were Craig and Susan, both with teenage children, driven, determined and planning for future growth. On the other side, was Damian, who felt that he had lost his enthusiasm for the things that used to get him up each day. He was reluctant to take the risk to set up another office in the US because of the economic climate and he wanted to be less involved in the running of the business. He was, quite simply, tired.

What the practice manager saw was a 'him and us' culture emerging at the executive level. Susan and Craig often complaining about the business being on hold. Damian complaining about being pushed. Interestingly, as an entirely predictable aside, revenues had stagnated for the last three years and staff turnover had increased to twenty per cent.

I was engaged by Susan, the CEO. My brief was to help push through the revenue block and reduce staff turnover. Needless to say, there was no mention of the communication challenges within the executive team.

How long do you think it took me to see the signs of the chasm? About thirty minutes! During our very first meeting, Damian had his arms crossed and showed very little eye contact. He was against the idea of engaging an external consultant who knew nothing about their business. 'Why spend the money? Why take more financial risk?' was Damian's response.

But by the time I got the call, the chasm was huge. It was full of angst. In fact, Craig was also suffering from a rare auto-immune disease and his hair was falling out in clumps, apparently related to stress.

Sound depressingly familiar?

This is not the first time that I have witnessed exactly this kind of situation in the last eighteen months. Here's a bit about the other organisations where I found identical problems:

A third generation family importing business with the kids wanting Dad to retire. Dad continuing to be involved in every aspect of the business and distrusted his kids, the youngest now being twenty-eight, to do anything right. He won't even take a holiday and sees himself working full time forever. His very first comment to me was 'They'll be carrying me out of here in a casket. The business won't last long after that.'

Another family business: Mum, Dad and all the siblings are on the Board. The middle brother is the CEO. The Board is not getting the dividends that they used to because the CEO is investing in growth. The growth has been forty per cent year on year and yet the Board has started performance managing the CEO because they want their dividends. It's got to the stage where the CEO is no longer invited to family events.

An accounting and financial services firm which had merged three years earlier. There are five Directors in the new entity. The memories of why they merged have dissipated. Board meetings are dysfunctional, the culture is toxic and the business — after only three years — is now running at a loss. The Director who contacted me is seriously thinking about just walking away and starting over. To top it all off, his wife 'needs a break' or the marriage is headed for the rocks, permanently.

A fast growth specialist IT consulting firm with five partners. They are all responsible for business development. One of the partners has brought $125,000 in revenue into the firm while all other partners have brought in at least $1 million each. The frustration in the Boardroom is palpable and yet nobody has had the curly conversation. It's the elephant in the room. The $125,000 partner doesn't actually know that he has a problem because he adds value to the business in so many other ways — in his eyes.

The office manager takes the call from the recalcitrant client. 'If that grumpy delivery guy ever steps foot on our site again, we are going to seriously have to consider finding another supplier.' It turns out that earlier that day, three drivers called in 'sick' and the founder of the business (now in his 70s) was steaming. He went down to the dispatch area, threw on some overalls and shipped the delivery himself! Obviously his grumpy mood that day impacted one of his biggest customers. And, that curly conversation has *still* not been had! What office manager would pass that information onto her boss's boss? And so the chasm begins, and deepens.

Please: Stop. Just come right on out and SAY it! Stand at the mirror and say it to yourself, out loud:

'The relationships between myself, my executive team and my Board could all improve and that alone would have a significant impact on both revenues and happiness levels.'

Woo-hoo! You did it!

But now what?

What's stinking up the place?

When we've built an organisation, we have made huge sacrifices. We've invested freely of our time, money, weekends, thinking, planning, doing. It's all encompassing, exciting, invigorating, challenging, frustrating, intimidating and every emotion in between.

When the going gets tough, when cracks start to emerge, we often respond the way that we think will best protect ourselves and the future of the business. This response mechanism is often heavily charged with emotion.

Over time, we become complacent, succumbing to the energy in the environment and allowing it to eventually become the status quo until the 'good old days' become memories and planning for the future is something that we're less enthusiastic about.

With our co-directors, communication can become anything from short to non-existent to actually oppositional or recalcitrant. Yet with hindsight, objectivity and a bird's-eye view we may well have chosen a different path.

I'm speaking from experience of course! Like any entrepreneur, I have left a line (a reasonably small line) of failed business partnerships in my wake. I certainly regret the way that I responded to stress in those partnerships.

I know now that I could have saved each and every one of them by leaning into the chasm. I know that *now!* And this is why I love what I do so much. It's also one of the burning inspirations behind this book. I know that disaster can be averted, if only we see the chasms, and act on them.

So, what's stinking up the place is the dead elephant.

And removing the dead elephant takes courage and vulnerability.

How many dead elephants are there?

The famous cliché, *a fish rots from the head* is something that I hear several times a week, and usually from middle management.

This week alone, I have heard about two high potential leaders who are planning to leave their current place of employment due to their lack of trust in the leadership team. Why? Same old, same old. Commitments not followed through, a change in priorities, mixed messages, a process-driven performance review, focusing on and measuring the 'wrong' things — the tired old oft-repeated list goes on. What it really comes down to is a lack of communication, leading to people feeling overlooked and uninvolved.

My experience tells me that there are often hundreds of emerging cracks in businesses. But people don't choose to actually leave until a chasm has emerged.

And here's another cliché I know to be true: people don't leave organisations. They leave their managers!

In 2013, the Edelman's Trust Barometer* released its 13th annual survey with the results from 31,000 respondents across 26 markets around the world — the largest survey of its kind. Some of the most interesting data is that only eighteen per cent of those surveyed trust their business leaders to tell the truth. Is this a failure of leadership? Yes, in some cases it is. But more often, and more specifically, it is a failure in communication.

To create a chasm, you only need to repeat your bad habits over and over for a while, whilst at the same time not hearing the feedback from your peers and subordinates.

In the early days, when the cracks are minor, you will get feedback, if you're open to it. It may come in the form of a joke, it may be an off the cuff remark or a passing, fleeting comment such as …

'Next time you want to address my team, could we discuss it first?'

'If you're visiting the client I brought to the business, could you please take me with you?'

'Can we stick to the agenda in our operations meetings?'

'You need to get your head out of the weeds more often.'

'Would you mind not taking any further calls so that we can finish this task?'

These comments made in the moment take incredible courage. And you, as a leader need to be ready to receive them.

Ignore them and the cracks become a chasm. Fast.

What's really interesting about this is that leaders are most often chosen for their courage, charisma and ability to communicate articulately and powerfully. But in my experience it's leaders who are able to *hear* these often fleeting critical messages and act on them that really stand out from the rest.

Being open to and acting on these messages, refining your leadership style and being flexible in your behaviour creates more open communication across all levels of the team and the business. And, the more likely it will be that people are willing to have the curly conversations — sooner rather than later.

> *It's as simple as this. When people don't unload their opinions and feel like they've been listened to, they won't really get on board.*
> —**Patrick Lencioni, *The Five Dysfunctions of a Team: A Leadership Fable**

Making difficult conversations work

When a colleague provides you with feedback and a curly conversation begins, recognise the choice that you have — you can recognise the chasm and peer into it, and try to cross it, or not.

In that moment, the most important thing to do is breathe diaphragmatically. When we're under pressure (for example, we know that what we're about to hear is something we're not going to like) our breathing becomes shallow. As a result, our anxiety level increases with extra cortisol and adrenaline released. So just take a moment to concentrate on breathing deeply as your colleague commences the conversation. Be open, willing to listen, and recognise the courage it has taken for your colleague to speak out.

Remain open and continue focusing on your breathing throughout the conversation.

Don't leap into defending yourself or argue your position; in fact, don't counter-argue in any way, until your colleague has fully explained what it is that's worrying them.

As challenging as this is, if you remain open, and you don't judge or defend, and if you thank your colleague in that moment, you are already filling a myriad of cracks that won't ever emerge.

Your choice to defend is a costly one. It erodes trust and creates politics. My definition of politics is a culture where people are careful about their language and actions, reacting with what others want to hear rather than what they really think and want to say. Politics creates a culture of compliance and a little army of 'yes' people making it almost impossible for you to attract and retain the innovators and entrepreneurs.

Is this sounding a bit dramatic? Well, I coach staff and managers at all levels to lean into these moments and provide the feedback to their boss *before* they hand in their resignation letters! Some people are more natural at this than others. Regardless, you need to be calm, present and ready to hear these pearls.

Are you ready? Really ready? Do you recognise how courageous someone has to be to tell you something 'curly'? Do you reward them with due consideration, an open mind, and a promise to think about it?

Attitude and influence

Attitude is everything. Because one person's attitude, good or bad, can have an effect on the entire team.

Years ago, I remember meeting a young office manager. During my introduction to her, her opening comment was 'There's something that you need to know and understand about me. I'm not a morning person so don't speak to me before 10:00 am'. And, what I duly experienced, day after day, was this grumpy girl whose belief was her reality, and everyone else's too. She spread discontent like a rampant virus.

She got a wake up call soon enough.

We all have a huge responsibility to ourselves and everyone around us to do a 'check up from the neck up' (as Zig Ziglar continues to remind us) and be cogniscent of the fact that our attitude determines our outlook and can positively or negatively affect our businesses. As a leader, attitude undoubtedly creates culture.

I received a referral many years ago to a large electrical engineering firm. I arrived right on time and the office manager took me straight into the CEO's office and left me to sit on the chair while the CEO continued his conversation on the telephone.

He was agitated, red-faced and aggressive in his body language. He didn't acknowledge me nor did he tailor his communication because of my presence. Mid telephone conversation while yelling at who I now knew was a service-provider, he said 'Hold on!' and looked across at me and said 'Are you Soozey? Do you mind if I swear?' Needless to say there was no opportunity to respond

273

before he proceeded to scream profanities down the telephone line. He was loud enough for all the staff in the open plan office outside his door to hear him.

Do you think I bothered going back there? I could have made money out of them, but I just didn't need to work in such a toxic environment for someone with such a destructive attitude.

Of course, the reason for the referral in the first place was because the other eleven members of his leadership team were not delivering! I wonder why?

It's what you're *not* saying, revealed by how you say it, that really counts

Attitudes are powerful.

Leaders set the tone. They create the fabric of the vibe that we all feel when we arrive at work in the morning — even if members of the leadership team haven't yet arrived, they are always present. They are the culture custodians.

Are you aware of the impact that you have on the culture of your business? Is it something that you are constantly conscious of?

Start being present, really *present*, in every conversation and interaction. Start listening. And showing that you are. If you are half-listening it'll be spotted instantly and resented.

A good listener tries to thoroughly understand what the other person is saying. They generate and create an environment of mutual respect.

It's easy to finish sentences, to assume that we know what happens in the end. A good listener listens intently until the other person has finished their thought.

There are lots of books, models and articles on effective listening available. You can go and do your research or simply just make a choice to be really present and engaged.

Don't jump to conclusions. Shift your listening antenna from that self-talk of whether you agree or disagree to concentrating on what the other person is saying. Are you sure you correctly *understand* what they're saying, for a start?

When we listen for agreement or disagreement, we're actually listening for trust or distrust. And we often assume one or the other through not listening carefully enough. So be aware of yourself and the attitude you are bringing to the conversation. Be conscious.

Of course, to listen to someone consciously, with concentration, we have to respect them. If you don't respect who you're talking to, you need to work that out first, or no conversation will ever be truly mutually productive.

In a workplace like the one I have just described — the angry CEO swearing on the phone while I was waiting — people would be constantly listening to him through a lens of fear or distrust.

So, what's actually going on for the listener is a second conversation (in their head) which goes something like this: 'Make sure to understand what he's saying so that we don't have a repeat of what happened earlier today. Should I write this down? Oh, no,

I left my pen on the desk. I'll just have to remember. Crap.' And their unconsciously anxious behaviour may come across to the recalcitrant boss as pensive, fluffy, disorganised, and unfocused. And of course, it's just a matter of time before the otherwise wonderful office manager makes one too many stuff-ups or chooses to work elsewhere. Somewhere less stressful.

Vulnerability

There's no such thing as the perfect conversation.

The aim of any conversation is *never* to miscommunicate — and yet so often what we say verbally, non-verbally and in writing can be — and is — misconstrued.

So, the challenge is to be aware and present enough to detect a crack, validate that it's there, and listen, listen, listen in an attempt to close it. It's about minimising the amount of time between what has been said and what could have potentially been misunderstood.

The Greek philosopher Zeno said that the reason we have two ears and only one mouth, is that we may hear more and speak less. Easier said than done, Zeno! In modern times the phrase is often quoted as 'so use them in that proportion'. It's good advice, and it starts with *choosing* to keep your head in the moment. The sooner we know that there has been miscommunication, the better chance we have of fixing it.

So getting back to the dead elephant. Are you able to articulate the problem? Can you see the communication cracks with the potential to become a chasm? In each of the examples in this chapter, the majority of members of the leadership team *knew* about the elephant in the room. They just had no understanding of how to address it. They didn't know how to even *start* to solve it. In fact, it seemed easier to suck it up, stay safe and get on with business than attempt to do anything about it.

Addressing the problem is about speaking the truth with empathy. It is as easy — and as fiendishly difficult — as that.

It requires you being honest with yourself and your own vulnerabilities. It requires you to leave your ego outside and lean into the conversation so that you're in tune, honest and aware of the experience that the recipient is having.

Brené Brown has spent the last twelve years researching in the areas of shame, vulnerability, worthiness and courage. In her book, *Daring Greatly*, Brené shares the quote behind her title. *Daring Greatly* is from Theodore Roosevelt's speech 'Citizenship in a Republic' which was delivered on April 23rd, 1910 at the Sorbonne in Paris. A passage from the speech is shared by Brené on the inside cover of her book:

> *It is not the critic who counts; not the man who points out how the strong man stumbles, or where the doer of deeds could have done them better. The credit belongs to the man who is actually in the arena, whose face is marred by dust and sweat and blood; who strives valiantly … who at the best knows in the end the triumph of high achievement, and who at the worst, if he fails, at least fails while daring greatly.*

We must be prepared to fail to succeed mightily.

I find that one of the most inspirational collection of words ever spoken. In a recent opening conversation with a coaching client, I shared some of Brené's wisdom. Tom was the CEO of a company going through a merger. He had some significant challenges with his Chairman that needed addressing and he spent at least thirty minutes dumping his concerns while I sat quietly, diaphragmatically breathing!

Tom's ultimate response to his Chairman? 'There's nothing in it for me to tell him the truth. I'd rather act naïve!'

That's so sad.

When it comes to vulnerability, we all need to step up and lead regardless of the size of our office, the title on our business card, the size of our car park, the length of our contract or our voting rights. Whether we are the boss, or a subordinate, there is no substitute for honesty.

We are none of us on this planet for very long. We owe it to ourselves, our businesses and future generations to courageously speak out with our truth and empathy, and especially so that the mid-sized organisations of today don't become the soulless, icy-cold corporations of tomorrow, and so that the icy-cold corporations recover their soul.

And how many of us have been impacted by or know of others impacted by the harsh cultures of global consortiums? Without doubt, every one of us has been impacted by their service levels.

'Thank you for holding. A customer service operator will be with you shortly. (elevator music.) Thank you for holding. A customer service operator will be with you shortly. (elevator music.)' Time passes.

Grrrr. Did it ever occur to you, Mr Soul-less Corporation Run By Accountants, to spend some of your mega-profits — generated by the very people you are now keeping on hold — on a few more people to actually *answer* the phone?

Committing to a cycle of honest communication

Honesty. Is there any better way to start a business relationship or partnership?

First rule: if you are unable to have substantial conversations with your boss and co-workers, go get some professional help — for you, and for them. It's not personal, it's business.

The inability to say the thing that will make everything better (because of fear of shifting the status quo) is a business killer.

How can you build trust?

In his book, *What Clients Love**, Harry Beckwith makes the point that in an increasingly complex world we require the assistance of experts. We can't always understand the complexities, so we need to trust our service providers.

Given a choice of providers, people are more likely to choose someone we get on well with. So people, and companies, with reputations of trustworthiness are more likely to perform better in the market.

As I noted earlier, companies with high trust outperform companies with low trust by nearly 300%. (Watson Wyatt's 'WorkUSA'*)

Do you want people to trust you? To do business with you *because* they trust you?

Well, to be trusted, first you have to be technically competent. That is a prerequisite. It's a given.

But to be technically competent is not enough — it is never enough — by itself. Internally, and externally, you need to be *seen* to be competent, to be able to communicate what you've done, why you have done it, and how it benefits your audience.

Next, you need to ask the right questions in the right way. Then you need to find the solution. You might ask your colleagues for assistance ('Who knows about XYZ issue? Who can help me?')

Having devised a solution, you need to present it in a way that makes it easy for your audience to grasp. This will vary according to the person you are speaking to.

Having offered the solution, you need to follow through, and persevere with following through. This is the area that distinguishes the top performers. You need to deal with objections, overcome obstacles, and gain agreement in writing for the work that needs to be done or the challenges that need to be addressed.

Having gained that agreement, you need to follow through and do what you have agreed to do, which requires technical expertise and we are back at the beginning of the cycle again.

And throughout this process there is a core competency: be personable.

You need to get on well with your audience. This requires several skills. Listening, observing, and communicating in the way that best suits. This will vary as your audience varies. You need to remain flexible. You need to alter your style according to the preference of the person you are speaking with. And you need to do this without apparent effort while maintaining authenticity.

Good communication builds good work, and both build trust.

Well-founded trust builds great businesses.

So here are some important communications attributes to consider when having curly conversations:

- How do I engage with my colleagues?
- What does my body language say?
- What about my tone of voice?
- Do I listen with my eyes as well as my ears?
- How do I check for understanding?
- How do my colleagues or customers measure my trustworthiness?
- What can I do to build greater trust?
- How do I cultivate lasting business relationships?
- Do I persevere? Do I follow through?

- Do I say 'Thank you'?
- What can I change about my approach that will make this company *great?*

Once you have got your personal presentation right, it's time to turn your head to the way you will strategise the meeting. Your first two questions should always be:

- Have I prepared for this, or am I going in cold?
- Am I sure of what I want to get out of this?

Setting the scene

Every curly conversation needs careful planning. Here are some guiding principles to assist you in creating the environment on path to achieving your goal.

1. You must have an AGENDA to set the scene for people. Use GROW to prepare your agenda.

   Be clear: what are you looking to achieve? How long is the meeting? What will be different as a result of the meeting? How will you measure success? What are your guiding principles — mobiles off, being on time, and so on.

2. Once you've stated the purpose for the meeting, finish your opening remarks with a closed question to make sure that your audience is clear on your ultimate goal. For example, 'We have been having some communication issues which may be getting in the way of our business success. I've called this meeting because I'd like us all to address these challenges as a collaborative leadership team. How does that sound?'

3. Make it clear what you *don't* want to talk about. 'Today, we don't want to get into nitty-gritty detail, I want to stay up at strategic level. If we do get off topic, I'd like to suggest that we "park" any other discussions for another day. Is that OK with you?'

4. Think about setting up the room appropriately for what you are trying to achieve. What type of mood are you trying to create? Who should sit where? If you are using audio-visual aids, make sure they are working before everyone arrives.

5. Who are you meeting? Are they Fast or Slow? People or Task-oriented? If you're meeting with a group, how will you adapt to suit all your audience?

6. Write a GROW PLAN. Write a plan for your meeting and unless there is a dramatic reason not to, stick to it. There are questions to help you prepare your GROW plan on page 256.

7. Rehearse. Now this may sound unusual — don't leaders just walk into a room and start talking? — but the best curly conversations result from having a well thought out GROW plan and the rehearsal for reality. Rehearse with someone who loves you enough to be constructive with their feedback! A word or two changed here or there can actually make a massive difference.

8. Remember, two ears and one mouth, used in that proportion.

9. Use predominantly open questions to elicit more information. Questions such as 'Why do you think you responded that way?'; 'Describe what happened, please.'; 'Could you please explain further?' Not only do these encourage people to talk, they also ensure that they realise they are being empowered to speak up openly and honestly. Don't be afraid to prompt with 'Is that really all?'; 'Are you

gilding the lily a bit?'; 'Don't tell me what I want to know, tell me what I need to know. I won't shoot the messenger.'

10. Be aware of your emotional responses. Stay mindful and remember the power of diaphragmatic breathing to both calm you and to display an aura of calm to your people.

11. Finally, do the 'check up from the neck up'. What are the top three areas that you need to focus on? Is it adapting your behaviour, sticking to the agenda, being comfortable in the silence, listening, respecting the other person, breathing? What do you need to stay mindful of?

Chasm closers

1. Acknowledge the dead elephant that's stinking up the place.
2. Determine the outcome you'd like to achieve.
3. Discuss the outcome with your key stakeholders (if necessary).
4. Develop your GROW plan.
5. Set a time for your curly conversation.
6. Rehearse your conversation.
7. Ensure everyone is really on board, not just playing lip-service.

If you hesitate to have curly conversations, go back to your WHY. Why are you here? What's driving you? That should be motivation enough to reinforce your reason for making the changes you need to welcome the opportunities that curly conversations present you.

Action This Day

There is a famous poem often called 'The Man in the Mirror', but which is correctly titled 'The Guy in the Glass', written by Dale Whimbrow in 1934. Its most famous stanza reads:

You can fool the whole world down the pathway of years,
And get pats on the back as you pass,
But your final reward will be heartaches and tears
If you've cheated the guy in the glass.

If you have read some or all of this book and you see echoes of your own situation in it, you have a crucial decision to take. It's a very simple decision.

Do something. Or do nothing.

If you do nothing, then you are willingly and deliberately surrendering your future to chance. And one day, sure as night follows day, you will look in the mirror and you will know that had you acted deliberately, with courage and with determination, to address the problems you now see so clearly, then you would now be looking back on a portion of your life when you were genuinely in charge, where you experienced the joy of working efficiently, effectively and co-operatively, and where your success was multiplied as a result. But because you did nothing, that didn't happen.

If you don't want to experience that day — the crushing realisation that you should have acted, and did not — then do some or all of what I am about to suggest.

Tricky stuff, change

I have walked into many organisations and the feeling of angst in the room has been palpable.

What they're thinking is blazingly obvious with their recalcitrant body language, paper shuffling, doodling, crossed arms and lack of eye contact.

Pfft … another know-all 'management consultant' who is here to try and change the unchangeable. We might achieve a slight increase in productivity but then we will all fall back into our old ways. The HR and Exec teams want change. But they don't see that they have to change anything. Anyway, my boss is an idiot. Ultimately, nothing ever changes. Still, it's a day away from my desk, I suppose.

As a leader, this is your biggest challenge (not mine). Your key role is to build culture custodians across all levels of your business. The culture custodians will build other culture custodians.

And all the while, your ego has to be left outside of the playing field because the ideas for change can't be seen to be owned by you.

There's no magic bullet in this book. I am proud of it, but there's no 'wave a wand and make it perfectly all right' in here. Those sorts of claims are ludicrously hyperbolic and rejected by intelligent managers, and rightly so.

What there is in this text is just loads and loads of really good common sense growing from decades of observation and real-world experience.

This is the most important thing I have to share with you.

Like the soccer story earlier, achieving a goal is a way of measuring the success of *every* player's input up to that defining moment. Even players who are at the other end of the pitch. Whose last contribution was a while back, maybe. Or who don't have a direct role in getting the ball into the back of the net. Every player on the field feels part of that goal.

Or they should.

There is a lot of good, solid research to explain and support why many change management programs don't work.

All of them are covered in this book — they boil down to a lack of commitment from senior management, lack of clarity in vision and values, introduction of too much change too soon, inconsistency in planning and implementation, poor evaluation processes and unclear measures of success.

The biggest single failing of any management strategy or change program is that *people don't feel they own it.*

Change is hard work and you need to cover every area — at the same time — if you want change to be sustainable. Hey, why do you think you get paid the big bucks?

So, start any change program with ONE thing. Start with chapter one. Start with your BHAG and get buy-in by getting everyone involved. Yes, it takes time. It also starts to create the kind of workplace that makes hard work fun.

Simple instant steps

- Read this book again and decide which section touched your heart and your intellect most, and why. Write down the most important items.
- Ask your colleagues to detail the one thing they would change about either you, the way the executive team works, or the company as a whole, if they could wave a magic wand and fix anything, instantly. Encourage them to be utterly honest and forthright.
- Give every member of your executive team a copy of this book. Ask for their thoughts.

A toe in the water

If you aren't ready to adopt the entire philosophy of this book in one mouthful, then do this, at least.

Consider, honestly and bravely, the impact of *your management team's culture and actions* on employee engagement and happiness, and choose one chapter from this book that will work towards improving that outcome in a way that enhances productivity, calm, enjoyment at work, and employee retention.

I am the Problem is designed to help overwhelmed leaders to put ego and insecurities aside, and have the curly conversations that improve long term business performance. You know you need to do this. Do *something*.

Act decisively as a team

If you're ready to act even more decisively, there is a simple agenda.

1. Step One. Admit that there's a problem. Tell your executive team, taking your share of any blame that attaches to you, and not sparing their feelings, either.
2. Determine where the pain is most acute and address that first.
3. If there's disagreement in the team, either over your analysis or long-term goals, then answer the BHAG questions in the Strategy section, but do it as a team, not on your own. Achieve goal alignment.
4. Determine your chasm-closing priorities, again as a team.
5. Agree on a plan to keep each other accountable, responsible, committed and on track. Set deadlines.
6. Start immediately.
7. Discuss, review and reassess as a team at least weekly.

Isolate the problem (and opportunity) with 'My business will be more successful when …'

When meeting business owners for the first time, my initial questions always relate to their definition of success.

Some of the classic responses include:

'My business will be successful when:

- we implement the new sales strategy
- we make the next acquisition
- we purchase the new Customer Relationship Management System
- we get the right leadership team in place
- we agree on an exit strategy
- we productise our services
- we get more venture capital
- we reduce our costs
- my ex-wife is no longer a shareholder'

(I threw that one in for a giggle, but it's a real issue right now for one of my clients!)

And the list goes on, of course.

So, let's start with you. How would *you* finish the sentence?

My business will be successful when …

The rule of half

Set out to be half right, sooner, and as a team.

Wait. What?

You need to understand this: there's no rule book for leadership, no perfect recipe, no easy wins.

There is, however, a huge amount of research both in the neuroscience and leadership space which confirms that the majority of working people like to make a difference and be part of something bigger than themselves.

In fact, it's the most important thing in their working lives.

That gives a great clue as to something every leadership team can do — immediately — to start bridging chasms and building an organisation that's sustainable, successful and a great place to work.

Start by creating some space to reflect, think, plan and communicate with your fellow leaders. Get right away from the office. Turn the damn phones off and insist you are not disturbed, no matter what.

Then, explain that your goal for the get-together is to get things half right. Get your strategy half right, get your vision, mission, values, budgeting and quarterly planning all half right. Get your marketing and communications half right. Get your innovation half right.

Get everything half right. Yes, you read that correctly. Half right.

Why? Because if people want to make a difference and be part of something greater than themselves, then you simply have to come to terms with the fact that you and your fellow leaders *do not have all the answers.*

Let's assume that you are really brilliant at your job. I reckon that being really brilliant at your job — if your executive team is the best in the world — means you have around half of the answers. I have never ever known a team with a higher batting average than that, and all the very best leaders of business I have known would agree with me.

What about the other half? Well, this is where the chasm closes.

The other half sits with all of your staff.

Especially the people who want to see an opening, step up, speak out, lean in and own a small part of what they're contributing to each hour, each day, each quarter, each year. The people who actively want responsibility. They want a bloody good reason to be a culture custodian, an ambassador for the business and a leader within the change as the business flourishes.

It's up to you and your team to create the culture of responsibility that allows this to happen.

It's the only way to unleash the knowledge and skills that are sitting under-utilised on the other side of the chasm.

When you've decided you're about half right, talk about who might have answers to the other half, and figure out how to unblock the pipeline so they can take some ownership of the situation.

The hard truth

No amount of training, listening or reading will change where you're at right now and get you to what it is you're working towards any faster.

Only action will make a difference.

And here's the real kicker:

It's more important to understand your constraints than it is to leverage your strengths.

As an 'adopted Greek' I have always loved the ancient legends of that beautiful country.

As punishment for trying to trick the Gods, King Sisyphus was made to roll a huge boulder up a steep hill. Before he could reach the top, however, the massive stone would always roll back down, forcing him to begin again. The maddening nature of the punishment was reserved for King Sisyphus for daring to believe his cleverness surpassed that of Zeus himself. Zeus, accordingly, displayed his own cleverness by enchanting the boulder into rolling away from King Sisyphus, consigning Sisyphus to an eternity of useless effort and unending frustration.

Thus it came to pass that pointless or interminable activities are sometimes described as *Sisyphean*: it didn't matter how Sisyphus strained every sinew and summoned up all his guile and strength; nothing was going to change the outcome.

Trying to make a 'step change' in the success of your business by trying to do 'more of the same' is a Sisyphean challenge. Or, as the well-known saying goes, madness is defined as doing the same thing over and over again and expecting a different result.

Yes, leveraging our strengths is crucial to business success. But without the curly conversations about our limitations, our weak links, our risks and constraints, we continue to operate like a three-legged chair. It's a relentless act that wears us down day by day and restricts our success.

Leveraging your strengths is just a starting point. Unless you predict and analyse those behaviours that have chasm-causing potential, you are driving your business in wet cement.

So, actively look for the weakest link.

Sit around the Boardroom table with your leadership team and ask the curly questions.

Ask the questions that will help you determine the health of your business *and* your role as leader.

When you find your chasm-causers, and you work out how to close the chasms, you'll find the success you're looking for.

You can make the changes you need to on your own. Just be honest with the Guy in the Glass, and get started. Today.

Frodo: I can't do this, Sam.

Sam: I know. It's all wrong. By rights we shouldn't even be here. But we are. It's like in the great stories, Mr. Frodo. The ones that really mattered. Full of darkness and danger, they were. And sometimes you didn't want to know the end. Because how could the end be happy? How could the world go back to the way it was when so much bad had happened? But in the end, it's only a passing thing, this shadow. Even darkness must pass. A new day will come. And when the sun shines it will shine out the clearer. Those were the stories that stayed with you. That meant something, even if you were too small to understand why. But I think, Mr. Frodo, I do understand. I know now. Folk in those stories had lots of chances of turning back, only they didn't. They kept going. Because they were holding on to something.

Frodo: What are we holding onto, Sam?

Sam: That there's some good in this world, Mr. Frodo. And it's worth fighting for.

—Lord of the Rings, JRR Tolkien

Endnotes

Thank You

Dweck, Dr Carol, *Mindset: The New Psychology of Success*. 2008
Ballantine Books Trade Paperback Edition Copyright (c) 2006 by
Carol S Dweck, PhD

Self Awareness

Dweck, Dr Carol, Mindset: *The New Psychology of Success*. 2008
Ballantine Books Trade Paperback Edition Copyright © 2006 by
Carol S Dweck, PhD

The 360° feedback tool I refer to is: Everything DiSC® 363® for Leaders
© 2014 John & Sons, Inc. Used with permission by John Wiley & Sons.

Achor, Shawn, *The Happiness Advantage: The Seven Principles that
Fuel Success and Performance at Work*
Copyright © 2010 Shawn Achor. Crown Business

Duhigg, Charles. *The Power of Habit: Why we do what we do and
how to change*
Copyright © 2012 Charles Duhigg. Random House 2012

Dean, Jeremy *Making Habits, Breaking Habits: How to Make Changes that Stick*
Copyright © 2013 Jeremy Dean. Oneworld Publications 2013

Godin, Seth. *Tribes: We Need You to Lead Us*
Copyright © 2008 Do You Zoom Inc. Portfolio 2008

Strategy

Collins, Jim and Porras, Jerry I. *Built to Last: Successful Habits of Visionary Companies.* HarperBusiness 2002

Lafley, A G and Martin, Roger L. *Playing to Win: How Strategy Really Works*
Copyright © 2013 A G Lafley and Roger L Martin. Harvard Business School Publishing 2013

Execution

Bossidy, Larry and Charan, Ram. *Execution: The Discipline of Getting Things Done.* Crown Business 2002

Collins, James C and Porras, Jerry I. 'Building Your Company's Vision'. Harvard Business Review 1996

Kipling, Rudyard. *The Elephant's Child*
Frances Lincoln Children's Books 2007

Buckingham, Marcus and Coffman, Curt. *First, Break All the Rules: What the World's Greatest Managers Do Differently.* Gallup, Inc. 1999

Dweck, Dr Carol, Mindset: *The New Psychology of Success.* 2008 Ballantine Books Trade Paperback Edition Copyright © 2006 by Carol S Dweck, PhD

Culture

Dweck, Dr Carol, Mindset: *The New Psychology of Success.* 2008 Ballantine Books Trade Paperback Edition Copyright © 2006 by Carol S Dweck, PhD

Energy + Mindset

Tracy, Brian, *Change Your Thinking, Change Your Life*
Copyright © 2003 by Brian Tracy. John Wiley & Sons, Inc. Hoboken, New Jersey

Dauten, Dale. www.dauten.com

Hill, Napoleon. *Think and Grow Rich.*
Copyright © 2007 Wilder Publications

Csikszentmihalyi, Mihalyi. *Flow: The Psychology of Optimal Experience.*
Copyright © 1990 Mihaly Csikszentmihalyi. Harper & Row 1990

Dweck, Dr Carol, Mindset: *The New Psychology of Success.* 2008 Ballantine Books Trade Paperback Edition Copyright © 2006 by Carol S Dweck, PhD

Shawn Achor, *The Happiness Advantage: The Seven Principles that Fuel Success and Performance at Work* Copyright © 2010 Shawn Achor. Crown Business

Gerstner, Louis V Jr *Who Says Elephants Can't Dance?: Leading a Great Enterprise Through Dramatic Change* Copyright © 2002 Louis V Gerstner, Jr. HarperCollins Publishers Inc. 2003

Self Management

Landsberg, Max. *The Tao of Coaching: Boost Your Effectiveness at Work by Inspiring and Developing Those Around You* Copyright © 1996, 2003 Max Landsberg. Profile Books Ltd 2003

Buameister, Roy F and Teirney, John. *Willpower: Re-discovering Our Greatest Strength* Copyright © 2011 Roy F Buameister and John Teirney. Penguin Books

Tracy, Brian, *Eat That Frog: 21 Great Ways to Stop Procrastinating and Get More Done in Less Time*

Communication

King, Martin Luther. 'I have a dream' — take the opportunity to read the full text of this speech at http://www.archives.gov/press/exhibits/dream-speech.pdf
Viewed 10 February 2014.

Gerstner, Louis V Jr *Who Says Elephants Can't Dance?: Leading a Great Enterprise Through Dramatic Change*
Copyright © 2002 Louis V Gerstner, Jr. HarperCollins Publishers Inc. 2003

Behaviour

Watson Wyatt's WorkUSA research can be found by visiting www.towerswatson.com

Brafman, Ori and Brafman, Rom. *Click: The Magic of Instant Connections*
Copyright © 2010 Ori Brafman and Rom Brafman. Broadway Books

Sinek, Simon. *Start with Why: How Great Leaders Inspire Everyone to Take Action*
Copyright © 2009 Simon Sinek. Portfolio/Penguin 2009

The work of Professor Tory Higgins, psychology professor at Columbia University, including Regulatory Focus Theory (RFT), can be further explored by visiting http://www.columbia.edu/cu/psychology/higgins/research.html
Viewed 10 February 2014

Curly Conversations

Edelman's Trust Barometer:
http://www.edelman.com/insights/intellectualproperty/trust-2013/
about-trust/

Lencioni, Patrick. *The Five Dysfunctions of a Team: A Leadership Fable*
Wiley 2002

Brené Brown. *Daring Greatly: How the Courage to Be Vulnerable
Transforms the Way We Live, Love, Parent and Lead*
Copyright © 2012 Brené Brown. Gotham Books

Harry Beckwith. *What Clients Love: A Field Guide to Growing
Your Business*
Copyright © 2003 Harry Beckwith. Warner Business Books 2003

Whitmore, John, *Coaching for Performance, GROWing People,
Performance and Purpose**. Nicholas Brealey Publishing; 3rd
Edition, 2002

Endpiece

Tolkien, J R R *Lord of the Rings*
50th Anniversary Edition Copyright renewed © 1994 Christopher
R Tolkien, John F R Tolkien and Priscilla M A R Tolkien
HarperCollins 2004

Glossary

ABCDE Method

A: Very Important and Urgent

B: Important

C: Good to Do

D: Delegate

E: Eliminate wherever possible

BHAG

Big Hairy Audacious Goal

CF'NO'

A Chief Financial Officer who is not engaged in overall strategy and sees their role as simply to refuse or cut back expenditure rather than invest in the business's key success-producing areas and people.

GO

Goals and Objectives

GOSPA

Goals, Objectives, Strategies, Plans, Activities

GROW

Goal, Reality, Options + What next?

KPI

A Key Performance Indicator is a type of performance measurement. Organisations use KPIs to evaluate the success of operational activities.

Multi-sensory learning

An instructional technique that combines two or more senses (visual, tactile, auditory, olfactory, taste) at the same time.

OH&S

Occupational Health & Safety concerns the safety, health and welfare of employees

P&L

Profit and Loss statement used to measure financial success

SEED

A method of delegation using

- Scope
- Empower
- Entrust
- Design

SHAG

A Smaller Hairy Audacious Goal!

SMART

Assists in creating goals that are

- Specific
- Measurable
- Attainable

- Realistic
- Time-bound

SWOT
- Strengths
- Weaknesses
- Opportunities
- Threats

WIIFM

Assists in communicating a message by reminding management to consider, from their staff members' point of view 'What's In It For Me?'

Further Reading

Barker, J R. *Next-Step Selling: A New Approach to Create and Deliver Value*, Longman, 2001

Berens, L & Nardi, D. *The 16 Personality Types*, Telos Publications, 1999

Bosworth, M. *Solution Selling: Creating Buyers in Difficult Selling Markets*, McGraw-Hill, 1994

Bourke, P. *Forced Focus: The Essence of Attracting and Retaining the Best People*, www.essencecomms.com.au Australia, 2007

Carnegie, D. *How to Win Friends and Influence People*, Pocket Books, 1994

Cialdini, R B. *Influence: Science and Practice*, Allyn & Bacon, 2000

Collins, J. *Good to Great: Why Some Companies Make the Leap ... and Others Don't*, Harper Collins, 2001

Covey, S R. *The 7 Habits of Highly Effective People*, Free Press, NY, 1989

Giovannoni, L C, Berens, L V & Cooper, S A. *Introduction to Temperament*, Telos Publications, 1990

Goleman, D. *Emotional Intelligence*, Bloomsbury, London, 1998

Hirsch, Gretchen S. *Talking Your Way to the Top; Business English That Works*, Prometheus Books, 2006

Hubbard, D W. *How to Measure Anything. Finding the Value of Intangibles in Business*, John Wiley & Sons, 2012

Isachsen, O & Berens, L V. *Working Together: A Personality Centered Approach to Management*, Management Press, 1989

Jackson, Maggie. *Distracted: The Erosion of Attention and the Coming Dark Age*, Prometheus Books, 2008

Johnson, S & Blanchard, K H, *Who Moved My Cheese: An Amazing Way to Deal with Change in Your Work and in Your Life,* Putnam Publishing Group, 1998

Jung, C. *Man and His Symbols*, Doubleday, New York, 1969

Kaye, B & Jordan-Evans, S. *Love 'Em or Lose 'Em: Getting Good People to Stay*, Berrett-Koehler

Keirsey, D and Bates, M. *Please Understand Me*, Prometheus, Del Mar, California, 1984

Lakin, D. *The Unfair Advantage: Practical Applications of Psychological Selling*, Lakin Assoc, 2000

McConnell, J V. *Understanding Human Behaviour*, Harcourt Brace College Publishers, 1989

Mehrabian, A. *Silent Messages*, Wadsworth, Belmont, California, 1971

Nelson, B and Blanchard, K H. *1001 Ways to Reward Employees*, Workman Publishing, 1994

Pease, A V. *Body Language*, Camel Publishing, Sydney, 1985

Pfleging, B & Setlin, M. *The Geek Gap; Why Business and Technology Professionals Don't Understand Each Other and Why They Need Each Other to Survive*, Prometheus Books, NY, 2006

Rackham, N. *SPIN Selling*, McGraw-Hill, 1988

Snyder, D P. *How to Mind Read Your Customers*, AMACOM, 2001

Stone, D. *Difficult Conversations: How to Discuss what Matters Most*, Penguin, USA, 2000

Tzu, S & Cleary, T. *The Art of War*, Shambhala Publications, Inc, USA, 1988

Waldroop, J and Butler, T. *The 12 BAD Habits that Hold Good People Back*, A Currency Book Published by Doubleday or Random House, Inc, NY, 2001

Welch, D A. *Decisions, Decisions: The Art of Effective Decision-Making*, Prometheus Books, NY, 2002